W9-AMM-761

SECOND EDITION

How to
Handle
Staff
Misconduct

SECOND EDITION

C. Edward Lawrence

Myra K. Vachon

How to Handle Staff Misconduct

A Practical Guide
for School Principals and Supervisors

CORWIN PRESS, INC.
A Sage Publications Company
Thousand Oaks, California

Copyright © 2003 by Corwin Press, Inc.

All rights reserved. When forms and sample documents are included, their use is authorized only by educators, local school sites, and/or noncommercial entities who have purchased the book. Except for that usage, no part of this book may be reproduced or utilized in any form or by any means, electronic or mechanical, including photocopying, recording, or by any information storage and retrieval system, without permission in writing from the publisher.

For information:

Corwin Press, Inc.
A Sage Publications Company
2455 Teller Road
Thousand Oaks, California 91320
www.corwinpress.com

Sage Publications Ltd.
6 Bonhill Street
London EC2A 4PU
United Kingdom

Sage Publications India Pvt. Ltd.
B-42, Panchsheel Enclave
Post Box 4109
New Delhi 110 017 India

Printed in the United States of America

Library of Congress Cataloging-in-Publication Data

Lawrence, C. Edward.
How to handle staff misconduct: A practical guide for school principals and supervisors / C. Edward Lawrence, Myra K. Vachon—2nd ed.
        p. cm.
Includes bibliographical references and index.
ISBN 0-7619-3814-1
ISBN 0-7619-3815-X (pbk.)
    1. School personnel management—United States. 2. Labor discipline—United States. 3. Documentation—United States. 4. School employees—Dismissal of—United States. I. Vachon, Myra K. II. Title.
LB2831.58 .L38 2003
371.2′01—dc21

                                            2002154032

This book is printed on acid-free paper.

03 04 05 10 9 8 7 6 5 4 3 2 1

Acquisitions Editor:	Robert D. Clouse
Associate Editor:	Kristen L. Gibson
Editorial Assistant:	Erin Clow
Copy Editor:	Robert Holm
Production Editor:	Denise Santoyo
Typesetter:	C&M Digitals (P) Ltd.
Indexer:	Pamela Van Huss
Cover Designer:	Michael Dubowe
Production Artist:	Sandy Ng Sauvajot

Contents

List of Progressive Discipline Charts

A Cautionary Note

This guidebook on procedures to handle staff misconduct is not a legal document. Rather, it is intended to provide information about the subject matter, and it is sold with the understanding that the publisher and the authors are not engaged in rendering legal advice or other professional services. Specifically, the recommendations contained herein are guidelines only, not legal advice. Moreover, the publisher and the author do not warrant, in any manner, suitability of these guidelines for any particular use. If you require legal advice or other expert assistance, contact an attorney or other competent professional who is familiar with the laws that pertain to your situation, and that prevail within the jurisdiction of your school district.

Preface

Principals have one of the most rewarding positions in a school district because they work with a sense of efficacy to operate a school where staff members teach and students learn. Moreover, principals have broad responsibilities to manage the school operation to improve student achievement and expand learning opportunities. In addition, they order supplies, equipment, and materials; direct pupil services, community relations, and financial management; and supervise, evaluate, and discipline students. Indeed, the principal has the challenging job of working with staff, students, parents, and community members, as well as with central office administrators. As a final point, principals also have one of the most complex jobs in the school district: dealing with the misconduct of staff members in school.

The second edition of *How to Handle Staff Misconduct* is written from the perspective of a former principal who understands the intricacy of the job. I was an assistant principal at a high school, middle school, and at the K–8 and K–5 levels. Also, I was an elementary and middle school principal. I must forewarn you that, during your career as a principal, you will have to handle misconduct action for inappropriate staff behavior.

When misconduct occurs, you must thoroughly investigate the situation, organize sufficient documentation, follow contractual provisions, and recommend disciplinary action. If you cannot substantiate that you met the standards of just cause and provided due process protection rights for the staff member, or if you do not follow contractual timelines, a third-party arbitrator may not uphold the disciplinary action that you recommend.

This guide provides a general overview of procedures that you should follow when a staff member engages in misconduct. Although it is impossible to develop a "recipe book" to deal with all allegations of misconduct that involve staff members, this guide provides examples of many misconduct situations. Even if certain misconduct cases have commonalties, the combination of circumstances is usually different in each situation. Therefore, before you use this or any other guide, you should thoroughly review the following: policies of the school district, policies relative to procedures for handling staff misconduct, files of past misconduct cases, state statutes relative to misconduct, and the contractual agreements of the school district.

Written in practical language, this guide gives examples of reasonable actions that you, as the principal, should follow when a staff member fails to follow district policies, school procedures, or your directives, or if the staff member violates the contractual agreement. You will find suggestions to help you avoid pitfalls you may encounter during the misconduct process.

Part I of the second edition of *How to Handle Staff Misconduct* discusses general procedures to handle school misconduct: Chapter 1—Strategies to Handle Misconduct; Chapter 2—The Misconduct Investigation; and Chapter 3—The School-Level Misconduct Meeting. Part II provides information about misconduct cases that the principal handles: Chapter 4—Unexcused Absence and Excessive Tardiness; Chapter 5—Neglect of Duty; Chapter 6—Abusive, Insulting, or Profane Language; Chapter 7—Corporal Punishment; and Chapter 8—Insubordination. Part III discusses cases of serious misconduct that require suspending the staff member from all duties: Chapter 9—The Immediate Suspension Conference With Hearing Officer; and Chapter 10—The School Board Hearing. Part IV includes criminal misconduct: Chapter 11—Sexual Misconduct; Chapter 12—Abuse of Controlled Substances; Chapter 13— Theft and Fraud; and Chapter 14—Criminal Misconduct Outside the School Setting. Also, a resource section was added to the guide: Resource A—Standards of Acceptable Conduct for Staff Members; Resource B—Letter to Schedule an Oral Reprimand Conference; Resource C—Major Components of an Oral Warning; Resource D—Letter to Schedule a Misconduct Meeting; Resource E—First Letter of Reprimand—Major Components; Resource F—Second Letter of Reprimand—Major Components; Resource G—Allegation of Staff Misconduct Standard Report Form; Resource H—Diagram of Human Body; Resource I—Misconduct Meeting at the School Level; Resource J—Misconduct Meeting With Hearing Officer; and Resource K—Letter to the Media About Criminal Misconduct.

This guide evolved through the experiences of the author and from the feedback of colleagues and principals during workshops and at inservice classes. At these workshops and classes, it became obvious that principals wanted a reference guide that they could quickly read to get a grasp of misconduct situations.

I want to thank the principals, my colleagues, and my friends, all of whom were my sounding board, for their assistance in writing the revision of this guide. I thank Myra K. Vachon, who was my coauthor for the first edition of this guide. Also, I want to thank my sons, Darren E. and Gary O., for their words of encouragement. In addition, I want to thank Lemmie, my wife and best friend, for her encouragement, suggestions, and critical review of this guide. Finally, I extend thanks to those at Corwin Press: original contact person, founding president and publisher emerita Gracia Alkema, who gave support and encouragement over the past decade; my current acquisitions editor, Robert D. Clouse, for his work on this edition; and the Corwin Press team that followed this book from editorial through the production stage. Thanks to Douglas Rife, the new president of Corwin. Also, thanks to Cheryl Williams, who helped format this resource guide.

—C. Edward Lawrence

About the Author

 **C. Edward Lawrence** is a Clinical Professor in the Department of Curriculum and Instruction at the University of Nevada, Las Vegas. He earned a bachelor's degree in elementary education from West Virginia State College; master's degree in guidance and counseling from Marquette University; certificate in administrative leadership and a Ph.D. in urban education from the University of Wisconsin–Milwaukee. Prior to his current position, he was the assistant superintendent for a large urban school district where he had an extensive educational career in public education. He served as a teacher; counselor, team leader, and assistant principal at the elementary, middle, and high school levels; as principal at elementary and middle schools; as director of alternative programs; and as community superintendent. In addition, he was a hearing officer for unsatisfactory teacher evaluations, second-step misconduct, and immediate teacher suspensions. In addition, he has consulted with school districts on how to prepare and win unsatisfactory staff member evaluation and misconduct cases. He is first author of the following books: *The Marginal Teacher: A Step-by-Step Guide to Fair Procedures for Identification and Dismissal* (1993); *The Marginal Teacher, Second Edition* (2001); *How to Handle Staff Misconduct: A Step-by-Step Guide* (1995); and *The Incompetent Specialist: How to Evaluate, Document Performance, and Dismiss School Staff* (1996).

Introduction

As the principal, you must know how to handle different kinds of staff misconduct. At the beginning of the school year, you must inform all staff members about policies, rules, and procedures that are designed to ensure the successful operation of the school. Also on the first day of the new school year, you should distribute and discuss a list of standards of acceptable conduct for all staff members at work (see Resource A). Each staff member should sign that he or she received the list of standards of acceptable behavior. This will help decrease the possibility of staff misconduct cases. When you provide all staff members with the foregoing information, you have met the first requirement in the concept of just cause.

Staff misconduct will interfere with your primary role of providing instructional leadership. Indeed, handling the misconduct problems is an extremely time-consuming, emotionally draining, challenging, and frustrating part of your job. If you have never been involved in a misconduct case before, you may become discouraged with the amount of time necessary to resolve it. Some misconduct cases may take weeks, months, and even years to resolve. In addition, the entire process may cost the school district thousands of dollars for legal fees and back pay to a staff member reinstated after a long suspension.

Frequently, when a staff member is involved in a first incident of misconduct, some novice principals may recommend termination or other severe disciplinary action against that person. When such misconduct occurs and you offer a more severe disciplinary resolution than used for previous cases in the school district, you may be accused of being unfair to the staff member because of race or gender. For instance, if a principal recommends a three-day suspension for a male staff member who swore at students but recommends a one-day suspension for a female staff member who committed a similar infraction, the principal may become involved in a legal battle because the misconduct cases were handled differently.

Under the pressure of the misconduct process, your success and survival may depend upon conducting a fair and reasonable investigation to determine if sufficient evidence exists to prove that the misconduct occurred. First you must base your decision to proceed with the misconduct case on firm evidence and the statements provided by the victim and the witnesses. Then you must carefully weigh the evidence and the statements. Before you render a decision, you must be convinced the preponderance of the evidence confirms that the staff member engaged in misconduct that harmed students, other staff members, the school, or the school district.

This guide is an essential tool for principals when handling allegations of misconduct that could lead to formal charges against a staff member. Parts I and II provide information on procedures that apply to handling misconduct such as failure to supervise the playground, hall, cafeteria, or bus dismissal; failure to attend staff meetings or committee meetings; and tardiness to work. Misconduct may also include the failure to pick up children at arrival, recess, lunch, dismissal to playground, or after recess or lunch. In addition, some staff member misconduct involves personal use of the copy machine, excessive personal phone calls, using the Internet for personal use, talking to other staff members across the hall or next door while students are left in the classroom unsupervised, or being disrespectful toward the principal.

Parts III and IV will also provide information relative to serious or even criminal situations that require immediate suspension: sexually related misconduct, misconduct that involves controlled substances, theft and fraud, and serious misconduct outside the school setting. Included in this guide are proactive tips to reduce misconduct, standards of acceptable conduct for staff members, an allegation of misconduct report form, diagrams of the human body, the misconduct hearing, and the major points of a letter of reprimand. Also included are progressive discipline charts to compare disposition of past cases in the school district in similar situations.

Part I

General Procedures to Handle Misconduct

Since contractual agreements differ among bargaining units, the misconduct procedures for staff members of those bargaining units differ also. In this guide, the sample letters are written for teachers; however, the same basic guidelines and content may also apply to other staff member contractual agreements. Thus the misconduct provisions of each contract should be reviewed in conjunction with this guide.

Strategies
to Handle
Misconduct

Misconduct is a confidential matter.

As the principal, when you handle staff misconduct, you must have a firm understanding of the concepts of just cause, due process, and progressive discipline. These concepts are the foundation for fair treatment of staff members in the workplace. *Just cause* means that you must have good cause to suspend a staff member, reprimand a staff member, or discipline a staff member. *Due process* essentially means that you show "fair play" in handling the misconduct situations. *Progressive discipline* is a series of steps in which you increase the disciplinary action each time the staff member commits an act of misconduct.

JUST CAUSE

As the principal, you cannot without good reason suspend a staff member, reprimand a staff member, or discipline a staff member. Some reasons to invoke disciplinary action are unexcused absences and excessive tardiness; neglect of duty; abusive, insulting, or profane language; corporal punishment; insubordination; sexual misconduct; illegal use of a controlled substance; thefts and fraud; and criminal misconduct outside the school setting. Moreover, you must be familiar with the just cause requirements in order to handle misconduct cases successfully, or the disciplinary action you take against the staff member may be overturned or reduced by an impartial hearing officer. To avoid this, you should review the "just cause" questions, which serve as the foundation for a third-party hearing officer, an arbitrator, or the courts to decide if just cause requirements were met. Arbitrator Carroll R. Daugherty developed a test in the celebrated Enterprise Wire case (46 LA 359, 50 LA 83, 1966). Accordingly, the documentation you present at hearings must clearly show how you met these just cause requirements.

1. Did you notify the staff member as to the behavior that was expected and the consequences or discipline that would occur if the staff member did not meet behavioral expectations?

2. Did the staff member know the rule, conduct, or procedure?

3. Was the rule, conduct, or procedure reasonable?

4. Did you make an effort to discover whether the staff member violated rules or orders of the school?

5. Prior to disciplinary action, did you conduct a fair and objective investigation?

6. Did you have substantial evidence and documentation to prove that the staff member was guilty of the misconduct charge?

7. Was the disciplinary action reasonable relative to the seriousness and nature of the offense?

8. Did you treat the person in a way that was consistent with the treatment of others who were disciplined for similar actions and under similar circumstances?

Meeting the criteria for just cause questions 1, 2, and 3 ensures that staff members know the expectations and consequences of their actions and that the job expectations are reasonable. Therefore at the beginning of the school year, give all staff members a list of Standards of Acceptable Conduct (see Resource A). Make it clear to all staff members that they are expected to abide by the standards. Also inform staff members that these standards are not limited to the examples provided on the list and that if they violate the standards in ways similar to these examples, you will follow through with disciplinary action.

Just cause questions 4 and 5 require that you must conduct a timely, fair, and objective investigation that gathers all facts and documents necessary to provide evidence of the staff member's misconduct. In order to fairly determine if the misconduct occurred, you must accurately assess the facts. If you wait too long to investigate an instance of alleged misconduct, you may damage your case. Moreover, if you postpone your investigation, an impartial third-party hearing officer, an arbitrator, or the courts may render an unfavorable decision.

With regard to just cause questions 6 and 7, you must provide substantial evidence and documentation to prove the staff member's guilt. As the principal, you must use common sense when you gather evidence to support your case and make a recommendation to resolve the issue. The kind of disciplinary action you recommend for the staff member should relate to the nature and seriousness of the offense. For example, you would not recommend termination for a staff member who has been tardy to work three times. Accordingly, when you recommend a disciplinary action, you must consider the following: the circumstances surrounding the violation, whether it is an isolated incident, the seriousness of the offense, the offender's past record, the staff member's length of service in the district, and the disciplinary action taken in similar situations.

With regard to just cause question 8, you must recommend disciplinary action consistent with the disciplinary action taken for others in similar misconduct cases. Although each case is unique, look for the commonalties and make comparisons so you can determine a fair disposition. Also, when you impose a disciplinary action, you must avoid making arbitrary and capricious decisions that could violate the staff member's right to substantive due process under the Fourteenth Amendment. This amendment guarantees that no state shall "deprive any person of life, liberty, or property without due process of law." In fact, courts have established that a staff member's interest in public employment may involve significant "property" and "liberty" rights, and these rights may necessitate due process prior to termination of employment.

DUE PROCESS

The legal guarantee of due process is in the Fourteenth Amendment to the U.S. Constitution. Simply stated, school districts cannot unfairly "deprive a citizen of life, liberty or property without due process of law." Due process, the concept of "fair play," ensures all staff members are treated fairly. As a result of Supreme Court decisions, due process protection for school employees is incorporated into state laws, school board policies, contractual agreements, and school district regulations.

Due process is divided into two areas—substantive due process and procedural due process. *Substantive due process* essentially deals with the question of fair treatment of persons by those acting under the color of laws, regulations, and policies in the light of our constitutional heritage when dealing with such issues as freedom of speech (LaMorte, 2002, p. 6).

Moreover, you must also understand procedural due process provision in the school district's master contracts. Specifically, *procedural due process* provides the right of objective determination of disputed questions of fact based upon established evidence. If procedural due process is followed, you reduce the possibility that a third party will decide that your recommendation for disciplinary action is null and void. As the principal, you must ensure staff members have the following rights during the misconduct proceedings:

- Notification of charges
- Opportunity for a hearing
- Adequate time to prepare a rebuttal to the charges
- Access to evidence and names of witnesses
- Hearing before an impartial tribunal
- Representation by legal counsel
- Opportunity to present evidence and witnesses
- Opportunity to cross-examine adverse witnesses
- Decision based on evidence and findings of the hearing
- Transcript or record of the hearing
- Opportunity to appeal an adverse decision

PROGRESSIVE DISCIPLINE

Progressive discipline is a series of steps in which you increase the disciplinary action each time a staff member commits an act of misconduct. Moreover, the goal of progressive discipline is to give the employee an opportunity to change the undesirable job performance prior to your taking disciplinary action. At each step that occurs before termination of the staff member, you should aim to resolve the situation without the dismissal of that employee. Depending on the seriousness of the misconduct, your documentation must point out that you started progressive discipline with an oral warning. It must then show that you gave the staff member an oral reprimand, held misconduct meeting(s), issued letter(s) of reprimand, suspended the staff member without pay, and concluded with the staff member's termination. As the principal, when administering progressive discipline, you want the third-party hearing officer to see that attempts were made to improve the employee's job performance. The steps in progressive discipline are as follows:

Step 1   Oral warning

Step 2   Oral reprimands

Step 3   Misconduct meeting

Step 4   Letter of reprimand

Step 5   Suspension without pay

Step 6   Recommendations for termination

For example, you should place the first letter of reprimand in the school file. In the second letter, you may issue a one-day suspension without pay and place that letter in the central office file. In the next letter of reprimand, you may recommend a three-day suspension without pay. In that letter of reprimand, you should include a sentence that states that if the misconduct continues, the staff member may be subject to more severe disciplinary action—up to and including termination.

Step 1—Oral Warning

An oral warning is the first step in the misconduct process. The purpose of an oral warning is to inform the staff member about rules, policies, and procedures that are being violated. An oral warning will help clarify the unacceptable conduct and explain the staff member's mistake—without issuing a formal warning. To help prevent small problems, such as failure to supervise students, from escalating into a serious misconduct problem, you should examine each offense and determine how the staff member can correct it.

When you give an oral warning to a staff member, do so in a pleasant voice, and use an "I" message. You, as principal, should say that you have a concern and need the staff person to help you to resolve it. Moreover, you must specify how you expect the staff person to follow through on your concern. Then, follow up this oral warning with a short memo. This will remind the staff member that he or she has agreed to help you resolve your concern (see Resources B and C).

Step 2—Oral Reprimand

An oral reprimand is the second step of the general misconduct process. As the principal, you must follow the proper sequence of steps when you issue an oral reprimand to a staff member for alleged misconduct. First, send a form letter to the staff member requesting a meeting in your office to discuss your concern (see Resources B and C). At the beginning of the meeting, you must inform the staff member of the alleged offense committed and then give the staff member an opportunity to explain. For instance, if the staff member continues to be late to pick up students after recess, provide specific dates and times.

When you listen to the staff member's version of the incident, keep an open mind. Occasionally, ask questions to get the staff member's side of the alleged incident. Also, you must not form a negative opinion about the staff member, and do not argue with the staff member. In fact, you may win the argument, but you may lose the staff member's loyalty over a simple misunderstanding.

After you evaluate all sides of the case, give a constructive reprimand; but do not lecture. Also, you must state as emphatically as possible that the staff member's conduct is unacceptable and that any future violations will result in disciplinary action. In this way, the staff member knows what will happen in the future and how to prevent another misconduct incident. Again, inform the person about the Standards of Acceptable Conduct (see Resource A) for all staff members.

Step 3—Misconduct Conferences

If you issue an oral and written reprimand, and the staff member continues to violate rules, policies, procedures, or the master contract, you must hold a misconduct meeting. Plan the meeting carefully as this is when you will discuss the allegations of misconduct. To verify what happened at the meeting, ask your assistant principal or supervisor to be present and to take notes. During the meeting, you must have a copy of the master contract on your desk. In addition, you should not focus on the staff member, as a person, being the problem. Rather, you should focus on the problem behavior at work. To substantiate the allegations of misconduct, you should present all evidence at the first meeting. That evidence may include copies of the following exhibits:

- Contract that was violated
- Standards of Acceptable Conduct for Staff
- Weekly staff bulletins, which have reminders to staff about rules and procedures
- Memo(s) sent to staff member
- Prior misconduct letter(s)
- Parental complaint(s) signed and dated
- Student complaint(s) signed and dated
- Staff member complaint(s) signed and dated
- Staff meeting agendas about staff behavior
- Duty schedules
- Bell schedule

When you present the foregoing exhibits at the misconduct meeting, you preclude a defense based on the staff member's being unaware of the rule, order, or procedure.

At the meeting, you do not have to render a recommendation to resolve the issue. Nevertheless, you must adhere to the contractual timelines when you issue your recommendation. Last but not least, keep in mind that a tape recorder, video recorder, or any other electronic device is not permitted in a misconduct meeting.

Step 4—Letter of Reprimand

A letter of reprimand serves as an official notice to the staff member. This letter summarizes the incident and the evidence and testimony presented at the misconduct meeting. Most important, the letter of reprimand provides you with documentation about the staff member's involvement in a misconduct case.

Your first letter of reprimand (see Resource E) for inappropriate conduct must follow nine important guidelines:

1. Write on official school stationery

2. Show method of transmittal

3. Describe/refer to the person's involvement in the incident

4. Quote the regulation(s) broken

5. Refer to previous oral and written warnings

6. Mention assistance given

7. State that this letter is an official reprimand

8. Explain the penalty for failure to improve

9. Sign the letter

Your second letter of reprimand sent to a staff member for inappropriate conduct will include eleven important requirements (see Resource F). For example, refer to the prior oral warning and previous letter of reprimand, explain the penalty for failure to improve, warn the person of the possibility of more severe disciplinary action, offer the person an opportunity to state his or her view in writing, and remind the person of the grievance procedures.

Step 5—Suspension Without Pay

If you have given the staff member oral warnings and oral reprimands, held misconduct meetings, and issued letters of reprimand, all without satisfactory result, you can recommend that the staff member be suspended without pay for a certain number of days. However, if records show that the staff member was suspended for one day for a similar infraction, you can use progressive discipline to increase the suspension to three days.

Step 6—Recommendations for Termination

If misconduct continues despite your efforts to correct the misbehavior, or if the staff member engages in criminal misconduct, you may find it necessary to terminate the person. After you present the misconduct case to an impartial hearing officer, the hearing officer can also recommend that the staff member be terminated. Furthermore, the master contract may include a provision that enables the staff member to request a hearing before a committee of the board of school directors or the full board.

The jurisdiction to hear and determine a misconduct case can also be held in state or federal court. In the state court system, you must be prepared for a challenge at the circuit court, the state appellate, and the state supreme court. Also, you could be challenged in the federal district court, the court of appeals, and the Supreme Court. As a principal, you must follow the strategies discussed in this chapter—just cause, due process, and progressive discipline—to endure a court challenge relative to how you handled the disciplinary action.

2

The Misconduct Investigation

Your best strategy is to prepare "airtight" documentation to substanti-
ate a misconduct charge.

As the principal, you must be aware of your responsibilities to conduct an investigation with regard to alleged misconduct. Although you may handle situations relative to misconduct, the police department with jurisdiction in some school districts will conduct criminal investigations. It is critical for you to work in concert with the police, your immediate supervisor, the director of personnel, or the attorney for the school district. In this way, you have their input and viewpoint about the alleged misconduct. Furthermore, it is important that you inform each person from whom you receive advice about the other advice you have been given in this case. Also, discontinue the practice of "shopping around," which is the unfortunate habit principals have of calling colleagues to get the answers they want to hear. Work together with your immediate supervisor, the director of the human resource department, or the attorney for the school district to complete your investigation and assemble airtight documentation to support the misconduct charge.

VICTIM/WITNESS STATEMENT FORM

As the principal, in order to start your misconduct investigation, find out if you must use the school district's allegation of misconduct form or if you can use the Allegation of Staff Misconduct Standard Report Form in this guide (see Resource G). This report form is used to gather facts about the incident from eyewitnesses and includes the name of the accused staff member, report date, date of the incident, name of the student or staff member who is making the statement, time of the incident, location of the incident, and who was present when the statement was taken. Each page should be numbered and initialed by the person making the statement to verify it, and the last page should provide lines for signatures, dates, and times. (The form in Resource G provides a sample first and last page of such a report.)

During the time the victim or witness is completing the victim/witness statement, the principal, assistant principal, dean of students, police officer, or school secretary should be present. The school secretary can write the information on the form for a small child or an older child who has difficulty writing. Because there may be numerous witnesses, they should be interviewed in separate rooms away from the victim. This will prevent collaboration in their statements. You may ask questions to clarify the incident, but do not coach the victim or witness to say what you may want them to say. For example, ask when and where the incident occurred, what happened, and the names of other witnesses. Do not use hearsay statements, which may not be believable evidence. Rather, make use of eyewitness testimony from those who have firsthand knowledge of the incident, which will strengthen the case. The principal should read statements back to the witnesses or victim, or ask them to read their statements, before all parties sign it. The victim or witness must initial each correction including spelling or grammatical errors, and sign the statement. As the principal, you must double-check the statement to find conflicting dates and times, and contradictory testimony, before presenting this information at the misconduct meeting.

DIAGRAM OF THE HUMAN BODY

In certain types of misconduct cases, a diagram of the human body may be helpful in taking a statement (see Resource H). Ask the victim or witnesses to circle the part(s) of the body and initial on the diagram to indicate the part of the body involved. The diagram of the human body must provide signature lines for the victim or witness, as well as for the people certifying that the victim or witness made the statement, and also school name and address.

POLICE RECORDS

In some school districts, the police department will conduct the investigation for criminal misconduct charges against a staff member. Always include a copy of the police report or criminal complaint of the arrested staff member for your documentation.

PHOTOGRAPHS AND VIDEOTAPING

You may also consider using photographs or videotaping the site(s) in the school building where the incident occurred. To help gather the facts about the incident, take as many pictures as necessary. In your documentation, be sure to include the brand and model of camera, date and time the pictures were taken, name of person who took the pictures, the date the pictures were developed and by whom, and who had possession of the photographs before they were presented as evidence at the misconduct hearing. In addition, you may consider using aids in the photograph, such as a ruler to illustrate the dimensions of features in the photograph.

After you complete your investigation, you must weigh the facts to make sure there are no gaping holes in the evidence, especially in the statements from the victim and witnesses. Be sure to review your documentation with the attorney for the school district or your immediate supervisor to determine if there is enough evidence to proceed with the misconduct charge. If not, this is the time to decide to discontinue the misconduct case.

Quite frankly, there are no easy answers or simple resolutions when it comes to a decision about proceeding with a misconduct case. To be successful in prosecuting the misconduct charge, you must follow the misconduct provisions of the master contract, and have airtight documentation to prove your case.

3

The School-
Level
Misconduct
Meeting

Be prepared to compromise on misconduct issues. Nothing is carved in stone.

To initiate the misconduct process, you must send a letter to the staff member to schedule a meeting (see Resource D). The misconduct meeting with the staff member and the staff member's representative will be the first official meeting to present and hear testimony about the alleged misconduct. Before holding the misconduct meeting, in your office or in a private conference room, you, and perhaps the assistant principal, should rehearse the presentation of the testimony. In addition, you must develop comprehensive personal notes to ensure that your presentation is well organized and that you include all the important information. Your notes should include an opening statement citing the misconduct section of the master contract and expectations for all staff members, reference to due process, background information about the staff member's employment with the district, and any previous disciplinary action taken because of misconduct.

When you conduct the meeting, sit behind your desk or at the head of the conference table. At this meeting, you should have a copy of the master

Figure 3.1   The Misconduct Meeting at the School Level

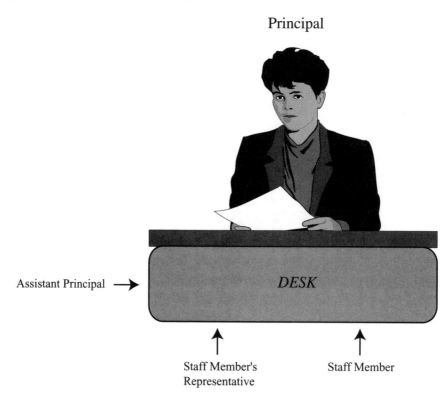

contract before you. Also, an assistant school principal or supervisor must attend the meeting to take notes and to verify what happened during the meeting.

You will clearly and concisely present all the evidence obtained during the investigation at the meeting. To prevent omission of important information, organize your notes so that the presentation follows a logical sequence. First, you will present documentation and evidence. Then you will listen to the staff member's response to the allegation. Although you do not have to render a recommendation at the meeting, you must adhere to the contractual timelines to issue your recommendation to resolve the misconduct. As a guideline to the seating of individuals at the meeting, consider using the arrangement shown in Figure 3.1.

The association representative, or an attorney, will probably speak for the staff member at the meeting. Before you proceed, ask the staff member to identify one person, either the representative or the attorney, who will be the official spokesperson. Also, set ground rules for other individuals who may be in attendance. Do not allow whispering, passing notes, tape-recording, or videotaping of the misconduct meeting. If necessary, take a fifteen-minute recess to allow the staff member and representative time to talk. Setting guidelines at the beginning of the meeting will allow you to recess without problems (see Resource I).

As you begin to present your evidence, hand out a folder to the staff member and his or her representative. This folder contains the documentation you plan to present, and each exhibit will be labeled. During the meeting, you can highlight each exhibit by saying, "I am presenting Exhibit _____ at this time." At the first meeting, be sure to present all evidence to substantiate the allegations of misconduct. In fact, you may be unable to introduce new evidence at subsequent meetings.

During the meeting, watch for the following examples of body language that may provide you with clues to the staff member's feelings: eye blinking; failure to look you in the eye; repeatedly taking off and cleaning glasses; rubbing the back of the neck, which indicates person is annoyed; perspiring; scratching the head; nervous finger tapping; loosening the collar; or fidgeting with hair or a piece of clothing. Although these gestures can be misunderstood, you may have some indication of how the staff member is feeling during the time that information is being presented.

After presenting your documentation, the staff member's representative must have an opportunity to present evidence and cross-examine you. Be prepared for the cross-examination to be confrontational in an attempt to upset you. Anticipate possible scenarios for the cross-examination. The staff member's representative will spend a great deal of time interrogating you about any inconsistencies within written statements of the victim or witness. Furthermore, if the witness and victim complete their written reports at the same time and in the same location, the staff member's representative may accuse them of collaborating on their stories especially if there are dates, times, or place contradictions. You may be accused of conducting a substandard investigation. Be prepared for the representative to try any measure to rattle you, even to the extent of marking your spelling and grammatical errors with a red pen and stating you are a poor example of a principal. It is important not to become angry during the misconduct meeting. Rather show grace and exhibit poise, and do not display facial signs that indicate you feel aggravated or guilty. Also be prepared for the representative to accuse you of showing favoritism, treating staff members differently based on race and gender, failing to clarify the rules and responsibilities, or any combination of these. Following is a list of common charges leveled at the principal by representatives in an effort to deflect charges against staff:

- Failing to follow state law or board policy relative to staff misconduct
- Failing to follow the misconduct section of the master contract
- Failing to provide an oral warning or written warning to the staff member about the problems
- Singling out the staff member from other equally culpable staff members
- Having a vendetta against the staff member
- Overstating the problem
- Violating the First and Fourteenth Amendments

Reduce the possibility of personal attacks upon your administrative skills by documenting and preparing your case impeccably.

To end the misconduct meeting, allow the staff member's representative to make a closing statement. Then state that you intend to review the information presented at the meeting and to adhere to the contractual timeline. Your resolution must take into account evidence that the staff member and the representative presented at the meeting.

Following the school misconduct meeting, you must weigh the preponderance of evidence to determine if the staff member's action was or was not misconduct. Then make a courtesy telephone call to the staff member's representative with your recommended resolution for the misconduct. Next send the staff member's representative a letter about your recommendation to resolve the misconduct. If a resolution cannot be reached in the first misconduct hearing, an impartial hearing officer will have to hear the case. The impartial hearing officer will examine the evidence in light of just cause, due process, and progressive discipline.

Resource J provides an example of the school-level misconduct meeting before an impartial hearing officer. Through a step-by-step narrative, this section covers the following: the opening of the misconduct meeting, acknowledgment of the master contract, and the agenda of the meeting (the rules under which the impartial hearing officer will conduct the meeting, due process, the allegations, the presentation of exhibits, cross-examination, the close of the meeting, contract deadlines, resolution, and the next step in the misconduct process if the hearing officer's resolution proposal is rejected).

Part II

School Misconduct Handled by the Principal

Part II discusses how to deal with staff misconduct related to unexcused absence and excessive tardiness; neglect of duty; abusive, insulting, or profane language; corporal punishment; and insubordination. Some specific misconduct examples include failure to supervise the playground, hall, cafeteria, or bus dismissal; failure to escort children to class in the morning, to recess, or to lunch; and failure to pick up children on time after recess or lunch. Still other examples of misconduct include a staff member using the school copy machine for personal reasons without authorization; excessive use of school phone for personal business; use of the Internet for personal business; failure to attend staff, committee, or department meetings; and tardiness to work.

For the principal, it is frustrating and time-consuming to handle such misconduct. Therefore it is important to take care of such problems immediately—before seemingly minor occurrences escalate to serious misconduct. Thus you must acknowledge every offense, no matter how trivial it may seem. Misconduct can be a single act or repeated acts. Also, the misconduct may be so critical, depending on the severity of the incident, that you may have to immediately suspend the staff member.

4

Unexcused Absence and Excessive Tardiness

If you make a mistake in handling a misconduct case, use it as a learning experience—not as an excuse to avoid misconduct situations in the future.

As the principal, you must be consistent in your treatment of staff members who are tardy or absent from work. At the beginning of the school year, you must inform your staff as to the starting and ending times of their workday. In addition, you should distribute a list of standards of acceptable conduct to all staff members. Include such information in the staff handbook, which should explain, in detail, the attendance and tardiness policy as well as the consequences for not following these policies.

A wise principal will always try to be aware of extenuating circumstances that may cause a staff member to be late for work. You will find, of course, that staff members have a variety of reasons for being late: car problems, faulty alarm clocks, or babysitters who are late or who don't show up at all. Prior to taking disciplinary action, therefore, consider the staff member's absence and tardiness record. When a staff member's record shows that there is a consistent pattern of tardiness, remember, it is the staff member who is responsible for correcting his or her absence or tardiness problems. The principal cannot be the staff member's parent. Finally, you must be consistent, always, in enforcing the absence and tardiness policies for all staff members who are chronically in violation.

If a staff member is frequently absent from or tardy to work, issue an oral warning. After that, warn the staff member—in writing—that any additional tardiness or absence will result in payroll deductions and that future absences and tardiness may result in disciplinary action. Chart 4.1 is the progressive discipline chart for unexcused absence and excessive tardiness to work. You should research your school district's misconduct files to complete the progressive discipline chart for the first, second, third, and fourth violations.

As the principal, you may have a more extensive list of types of staff absence and tardiness (e.g., doctor's appointment, car accident, car problems, head cold, broken glasses). Still, when a staff member persistently violates absence and tardiness policies, adhere to the administrative steps that follow to ensure a fair and consistent process.

Prior Warnings

- Give staff member an oral warning.
- Give staff member an oral reprimand.
- Give staff member a written reprimand.

Investigation

- Start an investigation relative to the chronic absenteeism or tardiness.
- Conduct an investigation to collect information relative to the chronic absenteeism or tardiness.
- Collect any supplemental documentation (e.g., board policy relative to the workday; staff handbook references such as guidelines for absence and tardiness; weekly staff bulletins that relate to standards for staff absence and tardiness).
- Compile a summary of the days and number of minutes tardy as well as the reasons the staff member gave for absences and tardiness.

Past Misconduct Files

- To obtain information about progressive discipline, review the misconduct files in the school and the district administrative office and consider the seriousness of the chronic absenteeism or tardiness in comparison to other misconduct.
- Before you recommend disciplinary action, review past misconduct files to ensure that recommended disciplinary action fits the seriousness of the incident.
- To determine whether the misconduct section of the master contract should be invoked, review the information collected during the investigation.

Chart 4.1   Progressive Discipline Chart 4.1—Unexcused Absence and Excessive Tardiness

Absence and Tardiness Misconduct	First Violation	Second Violation	Third Violation	Fourth Violation
Chronic absence (e.g., abuse of sick days, persistent absence)	Oral warning	Oral reprimand	Written reprimand; payroll deduction	Suspension without pay
Excessive tardiness to work (e.g., 5–10 minutes tardy two or more times per week)				
Repeated tardiness for duty (e.g., to pick up children after recess, lunch, or bus, or arriving late for hall supervision)				
Absence from work (e.g., leaving work before the end of the school day or open house)				
Late for class (e.g., in lounge using phone for personal business)				

Copyright © 2003 by Corwin Press, Inc. All rights reserved. Reprinted from *How to Handle Staff Misconduct, Second Edition* by C. Edward Lawrence and Myra K. Vachon. Reproduction authorized only for the local school site that has purchased this book.

- To find similar disciplinary actions against other staff members, review the district's misconduct database.
- Decide if your documentation related to chronic absenteeism or tardiness supports the allegations of misconduct.

Preparation for the Misconduct Meeting (See Chapter 3)

- Send a letter to the staff member to schedule a meeting wherein you will discuss the information that might lead to allegations of misconduct.
- To prepare documentation for the allegation of misconduct, place exhibits in order of your presentation.
- Prepare copies of all documentation for the staff member and the staff member's representative. Then distribute these at the meeting.
- Write out and practice aloud the opening statement for the meeting.
- As a guide, prepare personal notes to use during the meeting, but do not share those notes with the staff member or the staff member's representative.

Conducting the Meeting (See Resource I)

- Notify the staff member in writing of the meeting to discuss the misconduct allegations.
- At the beginning of the misconduct meeting, briefly introduce the meeting participants.
- Ask the staff member to introduce the official representative who will speak for him or her. If the staff member brings more than one person to the conference, make it clear that the other individuals will not be allowed to speak at the meeting.
- Cite the section of the master contract under which the meeting is being conducted.
- Specify the sequence in which the testimony will be presented.
- Inform the staff member about the specific misconduct allegation.
- Present all documentation to support the allegation of misconduct.
- Allow the staff member and the staff member's representative to cross-examine and to present any pertinent documentation.
- Consider any new explanation or extenuating circumstances that the staff member may provide to explain his or her actions.
- Interrupt the presentation rather than let the staff member ramble.
- Restate and clarify the comments made by the staff member.
- Be aware that the staff member's representative might try to put you on the defensive as a technique to deflect responsibility from the staff member, especially if you are perceived to have racial or gender bias. Do not take this personally.
- Close the meeting by telling the staff member's representative that you will need time to deliberate and that the staff member and the representative will be informed of the recommendation later.

- Assess the documentation and testimony presented at the meeting before recommending a resolution.
- Reflect on the information presented at the meeting.
  - Do you truthfully believe that an act of misconduct occurred?
  - Was a careful investigation conducted to obtain relevant facts about the misconduct allegation?

Evaluation of the Misconduct Decision

- Be sure to follow the contractual timeline.
- Recommend disciplinary action consistent with that used for other staff members at the school or in the school district.
- Decide if the "preponderance of the evidence" supports the allegation(s) that probable cause exists that misconduct did occur. If it does *not*, inform the staff member's representative that no further misconduct action will be taken.
- Decide if the "preponderance of the evidence" supports the allegation(s) that probable cause exists that misconduct occurred. If it *does*, inform the staff member's representative about your proposed disciplinary action to resolve the case.

Notification of the Staff Member

- Call the staff member's representative within the contractual timeline to recommend a possible misconduct conclusion.
- Move to the next step of the misconduct process if the staff member's representative refuses your recommended resolution. This should involve presenting the case to an impartial hearing officer.
- If the staff member's representative and the staff member agree with your resolution, write a letter of reprimand and place it in the staff member's file. Follow the steps in writing the letter of reprimand (see Resources E and F).

Next Misconduct Level

If the staff member and the representative disagree with your proposed resolution, move on to the next level of the misconduct process.

5

Neglect of Duty

*You must make tough decisions about misconduct. Is the misconduct
serious enough to suspend the staff member from the school?*

When a staff member fails to perform supervisory duties, it is considered neglect of duty. As the principal, you must provide staff members with a written description of their responsibilities, such as supervision of the playground, hallways, and cafeteria, as well as supervision of bus arrival and dismissal. When you communicate with staff members about their failure to supervise students, you must be very clear in your communications. In the weekly bulletin throughout the year, reinforce the Standards of Acceptable Conduct for Staff Members at work (see Resource A).

Additional types of neglect of duty are failure to submit grades, attendance, lunch count, and tardiness information or failure to attend school-sponsored events, such as staff meetings, committee meetings, department meetings, open house, or parent-teacher conference days.

While neglect of duty may be only a single act, it may be so serious that it will necessitate that you immediately suspend a staff member from all duties. Most of the time, however, staff member neglect of duty will call for progressive discipline: an oral warning, oral reprimand, a letter of reprimand. Continued neglect of duty calling for stronger discipline will mean you must proceed with a misconduct meeting. Without too much difficulty, you can usually prove neglect of duty. Nevertheless, in order to be successful in a misconduct hearing, you must document the incidents of neglect, use progressive discipline, and follow the misconduct provisions of the master contract.

Chart 5.1 gives examples of neglect of duty related to misconduct. An experienced principal may have a more extensive list of examples of neglect of duty. You should research your school district's misconduct files to complete the progressive discipline chart for the first, second, third, and fourth violations for any neglect of duty charge you intend to prosecute.

Persistent neglect of duty demands administrative steps that follow a fair and consistent process.

Prior Warnings

- Give staff member an oral warning.
- Give staff member an oral reprimand.
- Give staff member a written reprimand (see Resource E).
- Proceed to a misconduct meeting.

Investigation

- Start an investigation relative to the misconduct incident.
- Conduct an investigation to collect information relative to the neglect of duty incidents.
- Collect any supplemental documentation (e.g., board policy relative to the workday; staff handbook references, such as guidelines for staff and weekly staff bulletins that relate to neglect of duty).

Past Misconduct Files

- To obtain information about progressive discipline, review the misconduct files in the school and the district administrative office.
- Before you recommend disciplinary action, review past misconduct files to ensure that the recommended disciplinary action fits the seriousness of the incident.
- To determine whether the misconduct section of the master contract should be invoked, review the information collected during the investigation.
- To find similar disciplinary action against another staff member, review the district's misconduct database.
- Decide if your documentation supports the allegations of misconduct.

Preparation for the Misconduct Meeting (See Chapter 3)

- Send a letter to the staff member to schedule a meeting wherein you will discuss the information which is the basis for the allegation of misconduct.
- To prepare documentation for the allegation of misconduct, place exhibits in order of your presentation.
- Prepare copies of all documentation for the staff member and the staff member's representative. Then distribute these at the meeting.

Chart 5.1   Progressive Discipline Chart 5.1—Neglect of Duty

Neglect of Duty Misconduct	First Violation	Second Violation	Third Violation	Fourth Violation
Failure to attend school-sponsored events (e.g., staff meeting, committee meeting, department meeting, open house, parent conference)	Oral warning	Oral reprimand	Letter of reprimand	Misconduct proceedings
Failure to report to a duty (e.g., playground, hall, cafeteria supervision, bus arrival/ dismissal)				
Failure to submit information (e.g., grades, attendance, lunch count, tardiness)				
Failure to supervise students (e.g., classroom, recess, lunch, playground)				

Copyright © 2003 by Corwin Press, Inc. All rights reserved. Reprinted from *How to Handle Staff Misconduct, Second Edition* by C. Edward Lawrence and Myra K. Vachon. Reproduction authorized only for the local school site that has purchased this book.

- Write out and practice aloud the opening statement for the meeting.
- As a guide, prepare personal notes to use during the meeting, but do not share those notes with the staff member or the staff member's representative.

Conducting the Meeting (See Resource I)

- Notify the staff member in writing of the meeting to discuss misconduct allegations.
- At the beginning of the misconduct meeting, briefly introduce the meeting participants.
- Ask the staff member to identify the person who is the official representative to speak at the meeting. If the staff member brings more than one person to the conference, those individuals will not be allowed to speak at the meeting.
- Cite the section of the master contract under which the meeting is being conducted.
- Specify the sequence in which the testimony will be presented.
- Inform the staff member about the misconduct allegation.
- Present all documentation to support the allegations of misconduct.
- Allow the staff member and the staff member's representative to cross-examine and to present any pertinent documentation.
- Consider any new explanation or extenuating circumstances that the staff member may present to explain his or her actions.
- Interrupt the presentation rather than let the staff member ramble.
- Restate and clarify the comments made by the staff member.
- Be aware that the staff member's representative might try to put you on the defensive as a technique to deflect responsibility from the staff member, especially if you are perceived to have racial or gender bias. Do not take this personally.
- Close the meeting by telling the staff member's representative that you will need time to deliberate and that the staff member and the staff member's representative will be informed of the recommendation.
- Assess the documentation and testimony presented at the meeting before recommending a resolution.
- Reflect on the information presented at the meeting.
  - Do you truthfully believe that the staff member's neglect of duty represents misconduct?
  - Was a careful investigation conducted to obtain relevant facts about the neglect of duty allegation?

Evaluation of the Misconduct Decision

- Be sure to follow the contractual timeline.
- Recommend disciplinary action consistent with that used for other staff members at the school or in the school district.
- Decide if the "preponderance of the evidence" supports the allegation(s) that probable cause exists that misconduct did occur. If it

does *not*, inform the staff member's representative that no further misconduct action will be taken.

- Decide if the "preponderance of the evidence" supports the allegation(s) that probable cause exists that misconduct occurred. If it *does*, inform the staff member's representative about your proposed disciplinary action to resolve the case.

Notification of the Staff Member

- Call the staff member's representative within the contractual timeline to recommend a possible misconduct conclusion.
- Move to the next step of the misconduct process if the staff member's representative refuses your recommended resolution. This should involve presenting the case to an impartial hearing officer.
- If the staff member's representative and the staff member agree with your resolution, write a letter of reprimand for misconduct and place it in the staff member's file. Follow the steps in writing the second letter of reprimand (see Resource F).

Next Misconduct Level

- If the staff member and the representative disagree with your proposed resolution, move on to the next level of the misconduct process.

6

Abusive, Insulting, or Profane Language

School is a place where the students should find acceptance—not rejection—from adults.

As the principal, you must ensure that children learn in a safe, caring, and nurturing atmosphere. Therefore, you must have zero tolerance for staff members who use abusive or insulting language or who make degrading comments to students. Staff members who make negative comments to a student about the student's race, socioeconomic status, language, gender, ethnicity, abilities, or religion should be told quickly and emphatically that such conduct is unacceptable for a professional educator. It is by no means an exaggeration to say that such negative comments can psychologically harm students, perhaps even damage them emotionally for the rest of their lives. School is a place where the students should find acceptance—not rejection—from adults. So, it is important to protect our children from staff verbal abuse, insults, derogatory comments, or intimidation.

Chart 6.1 shows examples of misconduct relative to abusive, insulting, and profane language. As a principal, you may have a more extensive list of examples of abusive, insulting or profane language. You should research your school district's misconduct files to complete the progressive discipline

Chart 6.1   Progressive Discipline Chart 6.1—Abusive, Insulting, or Profane Language

Abusive, Insulting, or Profane Language Misconduct	*First Violation*	*Second Violation*	*Third Violation*	*Fourth Violation*
Verbal mistreatment of students (e.g., calling student derogatory names)	Written reprimand	1–3 days' suspension	3–5 days' suspension	Termination
Distributing school flyer with vulgar racial comments				
Making negative religious references				
Using gender slurs toward female student				
Using profanity toward school in front of students				
Using profanity toward students				

Copyright © 2003 by Corwin Press, Inc. All rights reserved. Reprinted from *How to Handle Staff Misconduct, Second Edition* by C. Edward Lawrence and Myra K. Vachon. Reproduction authorized only for the local school site that has purchased this book.

chart for the first, second, third, and fourth violations for any incident of abusive, insulting, or profane language you intend to prosecute.

When a staff member persistently uses abusive, insulting, or profane language, you should adhere to the administrative steps that follow to ensure a fair and consistent process.

Prior Warnings

- Give staff member an oral warning.
- Give staff member an oral reprimand.
- Give staff member a written reprimand.

Investigation

- Start an investigation relative to the abusive, insulting, or profane language incident.
- Conduct an investigation to collect information relative to the incident.
- Collect any supplemental documentation, for example board policy relative to the workday; staff handbook references, such as guidelines for staff; and weekly staff bulletins that relate to the Standards for Acceptable Conduct for Staff (see Resource A).

Past Misconduct Files

- To obtain information about progressive discipline, review the misconduct files in the school and the district administrative office.
- Before you recommend disciplinary action, review past misconduct files to ensure that recommended disciplinary action fits the seriousness of the incident.
- To determine whether the misconduct section of the master contract should be invoked, review the information collected during the investigation.
- To find similar disciplinary actions against other staff members, review the district's misconduct database.
- Decide if your documentation supports the allegations of misconduct.

Preparation for the Misconduct Meeting (See Chapter 3)

- Send a letter to the staff member to schedule a meeting wherein you will discuss the information that is the basis for allegations of misconduct.
- To prepare documentation for the allegation of misconduct, place exhibits in order of your presentation.
- Prepare copies of all documentation for the staff member and the staff member's representative. Then distribute these at the meeting.
- Write out and practice aloud the opening statement for the meeting.
- As a guide, prepare personal notes to use during the meeting, but do not share those notes with the staff member or the staff member's representative.

Conducting the Meeting (See Resource I)

- Notify the staff member in writing of the meeting to discuss misconduct allegations.
- At the beginning of the misconduct meeting, briefly introduce the meeting participants.
- Ask the staff member to identify the person who is the official representative to speak at the meeting. If the staff member brings more than one person to the conference, only the official representative will be allowed to speak at the meeting.
- Cite the section of the master contract under which the meeting is being conducted.
- Specify the sequence in which the testimony will be presented.
- Inform the staff member about the misconduct allegation.
- Present all documentation to support the allegations of misconduct.
- Allow the staff member and the staff member's representative to cross-examine and to present any pertinent documentation.
- Consider any new explanation of extenuating circumstances that the staff member may present to explain his or her actions.
- Interrupt the presentation rather than let the staff member ramble.
- Restate and clarify the comments made by the staff member.
- Be aware that the staff member's representative might try to put you on the defensive as a technique to deflect responsibility from the staff member, especially if you are perceived to have racial or gender bias. Do not take this personally.
- Close the meeting by telling the staff member's representative that you will need more time to deliberate and that you will inform them of your recommendation.
- Assess the documentation and testimony presented at the meeting before recommending a resolution.
- Reflect on the information presented at the meeting.
  - Do you truthfully believe that the abusive, insulting, or profane language represents an act of misconduct?
  - Was a careful investigation conducted to obtain relevant facts about the abusive, insulting, or profane language allegation?

Evaluation of the Misconduct Decision

- Be sure to follow the contractual timeline.
- Recommend disciplinary action consistent with that used for other staff members at the school or in the school district.
- Decide if the "preponderance of the evidence" supports the allegation that probable cause exists that misconduct did occur. If it does *not*, inform the staff member's representative that no further misconduct action will be taken.
- Decide if the "preponderance of the evidence" supports the allegation that probable cause exists that misconduct occurred. If it *does*, inform the staff member's representative about your proposed disciplinary action to resolve the case.

Notification of the Staff Member

- Call the staff member's representative within the contractual timeline to recommend a possible misconduct conclusion.
- Move to the next step of the misconduct process if the staff member's representative refuses your recommended resolution. This should involve presenting the case to an impartial hearing officer (see Resource J).
- If the staff member's representative and the staff member agree with your resolution, write a letter of reprimand and place it in the staff member's file. Follow the steps in writing the letter of reprimand (see Resource F).

Next Misconduct Level

- If the staff member and the representative disagree with your proposed resolution, move on to the next level of the misconduct process.

7

Corporal Punishment

Equip school staff with a thorough understanding of the laws relating to corporal punishment and the strategies for confronting and correcting student behavior in a firm but nonthreatening manner.

While students are at school, the adult staff is responsible for them; and the students are considered to be in the custody of the staff. In fact, it is a principle of education law in most states that the school staff members serve *in loco parentis,* or in the place of the parent. While some states have interpreted this to mean that school staff can discipline students as the need arises, including with the use of corporal punishment, most states have laws that prevent school employees from using corporal punishment as a means of student discipline. Still, state laws permit staff members to use *reasonable force* if they are defending themselves or others, protecting school property, removing a disruptive pupil from school premises or from school-sponsored activities, preventing a pupil from inflicting harm on himself or herself, protecting the safety of others, and maintaining order and control. It is crucial to note, however, that *physical force taken in anger is never sanctioned under the law.*

At the beginning of the school year, you must make your staff aware of the guidelines relative to the use of reasonable force. Also, you should give the staff member a list of tips that will help reduce or avoid hostile interaction between students and staff. You should also provide strategies that will help staff members keep their temper under control and that will assist them in handling an incident without becoming emotionally involved.

Also, encourage staff members to attend inservice training so they can learn effective strategies to confront and correct disruptive behavior in a way that is firm but nonagressive. Note that staff members may use reasonable force when working with emotionally disturbed students who may show violent behavior; however, the staff member must be trained in the acceptable techniques to restrain students.

Progressive Discipline Chart 7.1 gives examples of corporal punishment. As the principal, you may have a more extensive list of examples of staff members' use of corporal punishment. You should research your school district's misconduct files to complete the progressive discipline chart for the first, second, third, and fourth violations.

When a staff member persistently uses corporal punishment, adhere to administrative steps that follow to ensure a fair and consistent process.

Prior Warnings

- Give staff member an oral warning.
- Give staff member an oral reprimand.
- Give staff member a written reprimand.

Investigation

- Start an investigation relative to the corporal punishment incident.
- Conduct an investigation to collect information relative to the corporal punishment.
- Collect any supplemental documentation, for example board policy relative to the workday; staff handbook references, such as guidelines for staff; and weekly staff bulletins that relate to the Standards for Acceptable Conduct for Staff (see Resource A).

Past Misconduct Files

- To obtain previous information about progressive discipline, review the misconduct files for corporal punishment in the school and the district administrative office.
- Before you recommend disciplinary action, consider the seriousness of the corporal punishment incident under investigation in the light of misconduct files on past incidents to ensure that any recommended disciplinary action fits the seriousness of the incident.
- To determine whether the misconduct section of the master contract should be invoked, review the information collected during the investigation.
- To find similar disciplinary actions against other staff members, review the district's misconduct database.
- Decide if your documentation related to the corporal punishment supports the allegations of misconduct.

Chart 7.1   **Progressive Discipline Chart 7.1—Corporal Punishment**

Corporal Punishment Misconduct	First Violation	Second Violation	Third Violation	Fourth Violation
Causing severe injury to a student	Immediate suspension	Suspension	Termination	
Hitting/ slapping a student in the face				
Locking a student in a closet				
Paddling a student				
Pulling a student's arm behind the back and holding it				
Throwing objects at a student (e.g., keys, chalk, ruler)				
Pulling a student's hair				
Shoving a student against a wall				
Using excessive force to restrain a student				
Taping a student to a desk				

Copyright © 2003 by Corwin Press, Inc. All rights reserved. Reprinted from *How to Handle Staff Misconduct, Second Edition* by C. Edward Lawrence and Myra K. Vachon. Reproduction authorized only for the local school site that has purchased this book.

Preparation for the Misconduct Meeting (See Chapter 3)

- Send a letter to the staff member to schedule a meeting wherein you will discuss the information that might lead to allegations of misconduct.
- To prepare documentation for the allegation of misconduct, place exhibits in order of your presentation.
- Prepare copies of all documentation for the staff member and the staff member's representative. Then distribute these at the meeting.
- Write out and practice aloud the opening statement for the meeting.
- As a guide, prepare personal notes to use during the meeting, but do not share those notes with the staff member or the staff member's representative.

Conducting the Meeting (See Resource I)

- Notify the staff member in writing of the meeting to consider misconduct allegations.
- At the beginning of the misconduct meeting, briefly introduce the meeting participants.
- Ask the staff member to introduce the person who is his official representative who will speak for him at the meeting. If the staff member brings more than one person to the conference, only the official representative will be allowed to speak at the meeting.
- Cite the section of the master contract under which the meeting is being conducted.
- Specify the sequence in which the testimony will be presented.
- Inform the staff member about the misconduct allegation.
- Present all documentation to support the allegation of misconduct.
- Allow the staff member and the staff member's representative to cross-examine and to present any pertinent documentation.
- Consider any new explanation of extenuating circumstances that the staff member may present.
- Interrupt the presentation rather than let the staff member ramble.
- Restate and clarify the comments made by the staff member.
- Be aware that the staff member's representative might try to put you on the defensive as a technique to deflect responsibility from the staff member, especially if you are perceived to have racial or gender bias. Do not take this personally.
- Close the meeting by telling the staff member's representative that you will need time to deliberate and he or she will be informed of the recommendation.
- Assess the documentation and testimony presented at the meeting before recommending a resolution.
- Reflect on the information presented at the meeting.
  - Do you truthfully believe that an act of misconduct occurred?
  - Was a careful investigation conducted to obtain relevant facts about the misconduct allegation?

Evaluation of the Misconduct Decision

- Be sure to follow the contractual timeline.
- Recommend disciplinary action consistent with that used for other staff members at the school or in the school district.
- Decide if the "preponderance of the evidence" supports the allegation(s) that probable cause exists that misconduct did occur. If it does *not*, inform the staff member's representative that no further misconduct action will be taken.
- Decide if the "preponderance of the evidence" supports the allegation(s) that probable cause exists that misconduct occurred. If it *does*, inform the staff member's representative about your proposed disciplinary action to resolve the case.

Notification of the Staff Member

- Call the staff member's representative within the contractual timeline to recommend a possible misconduct conclusion.
- Move to the next step of the misconduct process if the staff member's representative refuses your recommended resolution. This should involve presenting the case to an impartial hearing officer.
- If the the staff member's representative and the staff member agree with your resolution, write a letter of reprimand and place it in the staff member's file. Follow the steps in writing the letter of reprimand (see Resource F).

Next Misconduct Level

- If the staff member and the representative disagree with your proposed resolution, move on to the next level of the misconduct process.

8

Insubordination

As the school principal, you must always conduct yourself in a proper manner, both on and off school property.

As the principal, you have the authority to set reasonable rules for all staff members. At the beginning of the school year, you must provide all staff members with a list of Standards of Acceptable Conduct for Staff (see Resource A) that are followed in school. Specifically, you must say what is expected, cite the policy or rule, and inform the staff that failure to comply with the rules and procedures, or to perform the required duties, can result in a disciplinary action. Of course, the policy or rule cannot violate discrimination laws or First Amendment rights (freedom of speech). Staff members who willfully disregard reasonable rules should be warned that they can be charged with insubordination.

Most insubordination cases are initiated because a staff member refuses to obey the principal's direct or implied order, but staff members who habitually ignore reasonable directives and procedures establish a pattern of conduct that can result in a charge of insubordination, especially if the staff member was repeatedly admonished about the pattern. Such may be the case, for example, when the principal repeatedly warns and gives advice to a staff member, but the staff member fails to improve. Before you issue a charge of insubordination, however, you must have evidence that the staff member knowingly and deliberately violated a rule, order, or directive.

When you present evidence of insubordination at a misconduct meeting, you must be able to show the existence of the school rule related to the insubordination. Then, you must explain how the staff member willfully disobeyed the order or rule. Moreover, you must show that this pertinent rule or order, which was violated, is within the authority of the school to make. In fact, as the principal, you must prove beyond a reasonable doubt that the alleged insubordination occurred and that it violated board policies, administrative directives, and rules of conduct expected of all staff members.

Nevertheless, the staff member's representative may argue that the staff member tried to comply with the order but was unsuccessful. Or the representative may present evidence to show that the staff member had a good reason for violating the order or rule. In addition, the representative may argue that the rule, procedure, or duty was biased or discriminatory against the staff member.

Progressive Discipline Chart 8.1 gives examples of insubordination. As an experienced principal, you may have a more extensive list of examples of insubordination. You should research your school district's misconduct files to complete the progressive discipline chart for the first, second, third, and fourth violations.

When a staff member is insubordinate, the administrative steps that follow ensure a fair and consistent process.

Prior Warnings

- Give staff member an oral warning.
- Give staff member an oral reprimand.
- Give staff member a written reprimand.

Investigation

- Start an investigation relative to the insubordination incident.
- Conduct an investigation to collect information relative to the insubordination incident.
- Collect any supplemental documentation, for example board policy relative to the workday; staff handbook references, such as guidelines for staff; and weekly staff bulletins that relate to the Standards of Acceptable Conduct for staff (see Resource A).

Past Misconduct Files

- To obtain previous information about progressive discipline, review the misconduct files in the school and the district administrative office.
- Before you recommend disciplinary action, review past misconduct files to ensure that recommended disciplinary action fits the seriousness of the incident.
- To determine whether the misconduct section of the master contract should be invoked, review the information collected during the investigation.
- To find similar disciplinary actions against other staff members, review the district's misconduct database.
- Decide if your documentation supports the allegations of insubordination.

Chart 8.1 **Progressive Discipline Chart 8.1—Insubordination**

Insubordination Misconduct	First Violation	Second Violation	Third Violation	Fourth Violation
Disrespect toward school principal (e.g., language, threats, assault)	Verbal reprimand	Letter of reprimand	1–3 days' suspension	3–5 days' suspension
Willful failure to follow a reasonable directive, rule, or order				
Fighting with a staff member				
Persistent gross defiance of authority				
Refusal to accept changes in teaching assignment				
Refusal to escort students to and from recess				
Refusal to leave room keys in the school office at the end of the day				
Refusal to let the school principal or assistant principal into the classroom to conduct an evaluation or observation				
Refusal to meet with the school principal to discuss teaching performance				
Refusal to report to class				
Refusal to teach a class				
Failure to grade student papers				

Copyright © 2003 by Corwin Press, Inc. All rights reserved. Reprinted from *How to Handle Staff Misconduct, Second Edition* by C. Edward Lawrence and Myra K. Vachon. Reproduction authorized only for the local school site that has purchased this book.

Preparation for the Misconduct Meeting (See Chapter 3)

- Send a letter to the staff member to schedule a meeting wherein you will discuss the information that might to allegations of insubordination (see Resource D).
- To prepare documentation for the allegation of insubordination, place exhibits in order of your presentation.
- Prepare copies of all documentation for the staff member and the staff member's representative. Then distribute these at the meeting.
- Write out and practice aloud the opening statement for the meeting.
- As a guide, prepare personal notes to use during the meeting, but do not share those notes with the staff member or the staff member's representative.

Conducting the Meeting (See Resource I)

- Notify the staff member in writing of the meeting to discuss the insubordination allegations.
- At the beginning of the misconduct meeting, briefly introduce the meeting participants.
- Ask the staff member to identify the person who is the official representative to speak at the meeting. If the staff member brings more than one person to the conference, only the official representative will be allowed to speak at the meeting.
- Cite the section of the master contract under which the meeting is being conducted.
- Specify the sequence in which the testimony will be presented.
- Inform the staff member about the insubordination allegation.
- Present all documentation to support the allegations of insubordination.
- Allow the staff member and the staff member's representative to cross-examine and to present any pertinent documentation.
- Consider any new explanation of extenuating circumstances that the staff member may present to explain his or her actions.
- Interrupt the presentation rather than let the staff member ramble.
- Restate and clarify the comments made by the staff member.
- Be aware that the staff member's representative might try to put you on the defensive as a technique to deflect responsibility from the staff member, especially if you are perceived to have racial or gender bias. Do not take this personally.
- Close the meeting by telling the staff member's representative that you will need time to deliberate and they will be informed of the recommendation.
- Assess the documentation and testimony presented at the meeting before recommending a resolution.
- Reflect on the information presented at the meeting.
  - Do you truthfully believe that an act of insubordination occurred?
  - Was a careful investigation conducted to obtain relevant facts about the insubordination allegation?

Evaluation of the Misconduct Decision

- Be sure to follow the contractual timeline.
- Recommend disciplinary action consistent with that used for other staff members at the school or in the school district.
- Decide if the "preponderance of the evidence" supports the allegation(s) that probable cause exists that insubordination did occur. If it does *not*, inform the staff member's representative that no further misconduct action will be taken.
- Decide if the "preponderance of the evidence" supports the allegation(s) that probable cause exists that insubordination occurred. If it *does*, inform the staff member's representative about your proposed disciplinary action to resolve the case.

Notification of the Staff Member

- Call the staff member's representative within the contractual timeline to recommend a possible misconduct conclusion.
- Move to the next step of the misconduct process if the staff member's representative refuses your recommended resolution. This should involve presenting the case to an impartial hearing officer (see Resource J).
- If the staff member's representative and the staff member agree with your resolution, write a letter of reprimand and place it in the staff member's file. Follow the steps in writing the letter of reprimand (see Resource F).

Next Misconduct Level

- If the staff member and the representative disagree with your proposed resolution, move on to the next level of the misconduct process.

Part III

Serious Misconduct Requiring Immediate Suspension

When an allegation of serious, or criminal, misconduct is made against the staff member, an immediate suspension is appropriate. Serious misconduct includes allegations such as theft, sexual relationship with a student, insubordination, gross racial slurs directed at students, or fighting with another staff member in the presence of students. If a staff member is alleged to have committed such serious misconduct, immediate suspension may be appropriate. Depending upon the seriousness of the incident, you may also have to immediately suspend a staff member for misconduct that is unacceptable behavior, such as excessive tardiness, failure to supervise students, inciting a student walkout, or hitting a student.

A resolution for criminal misconduct is rarely reached at the school level. You should plan to move to the next level of the misconduct process. In some instances, a court hearing may be a collateral hearing, if the misconduct involves a criminal act inside or outside of the school setting. Since some misconduct cases take three or more years to settle, it is difficult to remember all of the facts. This gives the defense an advantage because witnesses may not be able to recall details, may have moved, or may even have died. Therefore, you must immediately begin the process of documentation with accurate notes and complete files of reports from witnesses and the victim.

9

The Immediate Suspension Conference With Hearing Officer

To begin the immediate suspension misconduct process, inform your supervisor about the allegation of serious misconduct. Together, you and your supervisor will decide if there is sufficient evidence to justify the immediate suspension of the staff member with pay. Also, the staff member's contract specifies the number of school days that you can suspend the staff member with pay. This time is allotted so you can complete an investigation about the alleged misconduct.

To release the staff member from duties, the school district must issue a letter written by an administrator at the district office. In addition, the district administrator should make a courtesy telephone call to the staff member's association to inform them of the immediate suspension. When the suspension letter is issued to the staff member, the association may send a representative to the school to be present when the letter is issued.

During the investigation, if there is criminal misconduct, the police department that has jurisdiction in the school district may gather information

Figure 9.1   The District-Level Misconduct Conference With Hearing Officer

Hearing Officer

Staff Member's Representative →   *Conference Table*   ← Principal

Staff Member

about the allegation. Nevertheless, you must also compile the documentation and testimony with regard to the alleged misconduct.

You will work with the school district's media specialist to prepare a press release and may be called upon by the media to answer questions. Remember, however, personnel matters are extremely confidential. Reporters should be referred to the individual the district has designated as spokesperson, usually the media specialist or the chief school officer (e.g., the superintendent). (See Resource K, Letter to the Media About Criminal Misconduct.)

At the meeting for immediate suspension, both sides will present their statements to the hearing officer. First, the principal presents; then the staff member's representative presents for the staff member. When you make your presentation, always speak directly to the hearing officer and make eye contact. Your goal is to convince the hearing officer that your documentation will substantiate the misconduct allegations. You are not trying to convince the staff member and the representative that the staff member's behavior was unacceptable.

At this hearing, try not to allow the staff member or the representative to distract you. In fact, they may not even look at you during your presentation. Instead, they will probably be looking at the hearing officer or taking notes about your presentation. An example of the seating arrangement for a presentation to an impartial hearing officer is shown in Figure 9.1.

The impartial hearing officer will follow the timeline specified in the master contract and send a letter to the staff member that will recommend a resolution to the misconduct. The recommendation may be to dismiss the case, to reduce the disciplinary action recommended by the principal, to uphold the principal's recommendation, or to recommend termination of the staff member. Resource J provides a sample narrative of a misconduct case presented to an impartial hearing officer.

10

The School
Board Hearing

If the hearing officer recommends that the misconduct investigation proceed to the board of education level of the process for possible termination of the staff member, the director of personnel sends a letter to the superintendent of schools about the case. If the superintendent of schools concurs with the recommendation for termination, the director of personnel sends a letter informing the staff member that the board of education will hold a hearing on the allegation of misconduct. Moreover, each board member should be questioned to ascertain, for the public record, that no relationship with the staff member exists that would prevent the board member from functioning as an impartial judge for this misconduct case. A board member who is unable to be impartial should be excused from the case. Then the board hears the case to decide if the staff member is guilty beyond a reasonable doubt.

The attorney for the school district and the attorney for the staff member usually present their cases to the board of education. At the hearing, the staff member's attorney will have access to all evidence as well as to the names of witnesses, including students, who provided written statements. The questions directed to the principal usually require a yes or no answer. Also, for the first time in the process, the attorney for the staff member has an opportunity to cross-examine all witnesses. The decision of the board of education is based on the evidence and testimony of this hearing. A full transcript or record is made of the hearing and is available for the staff member.

Following the hearing, the board has several possible options to resolve the misconduct. They can dismiss the case, reduce the disciplinary action, or concur with the termination recommendation. If the board of education recommends termination, the director of personnel sends a letter to the staff member. This letter then confirms the board's decision to terminate the staff member's employment with the school district. In addition, this letter outlines the grievance procedure, which gives the staff member an opportunity to appeal the board's decision, usually to an arbitrator. The arbitrator's decision is final and binding on the board, the staff member's association, and the staff member.

Part IV

Criminal Misconduct

Part IV discusses the criminal misconduct of a staff member. Such misconduct may include involvement in a sexual relationship with a student, possession of drugs or alcohol, or fraud and theft. When criminal allegations are made against a staff member, you must immediately suspend that staff member with pay. During the period of suspension, you must conduct a thorough investigation of the alleged incident(s) to present testimony and documentation to the hearing officer or board of education.

11

Sexual Misconduct

Rumor and idle speculation, of course, are not uncommon and will never be enough to uphold the staff member's termination; but when a staff member is proven to be involved in sexual misconduct, that staff member should face dismissal from the school district and revocation of license.

One of the most serious forms of misconduct a school administrator must deal with is the sexual involvement of a staff member with a student. However, allegations of sexual misconduct must be proven. There must be evidence that the staff member was sexually involved with a student. Rumor and idle speculation, of course, are not uncommon and will never be enough to uphold the staff member's dismissal, the nonrenewal of a contract, or the revocation of a license. Also, keep in mind that an allegation of sexual misconduct will damage the professional reputation and future employment opportunities of the staff member. Furthermore, you must prove that sexual involvement has had a detrimental effect upon the staff member's ability to teach or to supervise students.

State law describes sexually related behavior and the consequences for staff members who violate the law. In addition, the school board should have a policy stating that it is committed to the professional behavior of all district staff members. Then, at the misconduct meeting, you should quote state statutes and board policy that refer to staff members who have a sexual relationship with students. A staff member who is involved in such misconduct should face dismissal from the school district and revocation of license.

When a student, parent, or staff member informs you about an alleged inappropriate sexual incident that involves a staff member, you must act immediately. Call your immediate supervisor, the personnel director, and the pubic relations specialist for the district. If the three of you agree, call the police department. Regardless of whether the sexually related incident is the first violation or an isolated incident, you must immediately suspend (with pay) the staff member pending an investigation.

Progressive Discipline Chart 11.1 provides examples of sexual misconduct. You should research your school district's misconduct files to complete the progressive discipline chart for the first, second, third, and fourth violations.

The following steps should be taken for allegations of criminal misconduct for sexually related misconduct:

Speak to Personnel at the
Central Administration Office Immediately

- Call your immediate supervisor.
- Call the public relations specialist for the district.
- Call the director of personnel for the district.
- If the three of you agree, call the police department.

Investigation

- Start an investigation relative to the misconduct incident and assist the police agency with jurisdiction in your school district to conduct an investigation.
- Use a standard form to collect statements from all witnesses and other individuals—including the parents—and others who may have information about the alleged incident. This may include students, staff, and secretaries. This will help ensure that the information is more accurate and complete (see Resource G). Remind the witnesses and victim to be specific and to include the following:
  - Where (location or area in which the incident occurred)
  - When (date and time)
  - Who (first and last names of people involved or who were witnesses, if known)
  - What (the events and actions that occurred)
- Interview witnesses separately and follow up with pointed questions. Probe witnesses to ensure that all information is accurate and complete.
- Thoroughly read statements to see if there are any inaccuracies, such as dates or times.
- If necessary, use the body diagram to show the parts of the body involved in this incident (see Resource H).
- If necessary, draw a diagram that shows where the incident occurred and any movement of persons involved.

Chart 11.1 **Progressive Discipline Chart 11.1—Sexual Misconduct**

Sexual Misconduct	First Violation	Second Violation	Third Violation	Fourth Violation
Being involved in a heterosexual act or acts with a student	Immediate suspension; termination			
Being involved in a homosexual relationship with a student				
Exposing self to students				
Describing sexual activities between adults				
Engaging in sexual harassment of a female or male staff member				
Improper sexual behavior toward students				
Inappropriate sexual comments to students				
Inappropriately touching a student for sexual gratification (e.g., legs, breast, buttocks, knee, ears, back)				
Kissing a student				
Rubbing, touching, or fondling student's private parts				
Sexual intercourse with a student				
Sexual molestation of a student				
Sexually abusive conduct toward a student				
Showing an obscene or X-rated film to students				
Showing pornographic materials to students				
Telling sexually related jokes to students, in or outside the classroom				
Touching a student improperly				
Using obscene gestures toward students				
Using sexually explicit language with a student, in or outside the classroom				
Using sexually related materials in the classroom				
Writing sexually explicit poems in class				

Copyright © 2003 by Corwin Press, Inc. All rights reserved. Reprinted from *How to Handle Staff Misconduct, Second Edition* by C. Edward Lawrence and Myra K. Vachon. Reproduction authorized only for the local school site that has purchased this book.

- If necessary, use photographs or videotapes of the classroom or area where the incident occurred.
- Contact law enforcement agencies (e.g., police, sheriff, FBI), for a copy of the police report and statement of charges.
- Collect any supplemental documentation. This documentation may include board policy relative to the workday; staff handbook references, such as guidelines for student supervision and standards for staff; and weekly bulletin references to the Standards for Acceptable Conduct (see Resource A).

Past Misconduct Files

- To obtain information about progressive discipline, review the misconduct files in the school and the district administrative office.
- Before you recommend disciplinary action, review misconduct files to ensure that the recommended disciplinary action fits the seriousness of the incident.
- Review the information collected during the investigation to determine whether the misconduct section of the master contract should be invoked.
- Review the district's misconduct database to find similar disciplinary actions against other staff members.
- Decide if your documentation supports the allegations of sexual misconduct.

Preparation for the Misconduct Meeting
With the Hearing Officer (See Chapter 9)

- Send a letter to the staff member to schedule a meeting wherein you will discuss the information that might lead to allegations of sexual misconduct.
- When you prepare documentation for the allegation of sexual misconduct, place exhibits in the order you will present them.
- Prepare copies of all documentation for the staff member and the staff member's representative. Then distribute these at the meeting.
- Write out and practice aloud the opening statement for the meeting.
- Prepare personal notes to use as a guide during the meeting, but do not share those notes with the staff member or the staff member's representative.

Meeting Conducted by the Hearing Officer (See Resource J)

- Before the hearing officer begins the misconduct meeting, briefly introduce the participants.
- The hearing officer will ask the staff member to identify the person who is the official representative to speak at the meeting. If the staff member brings more than one person to the conference, only the official representative will be allowed to speak.

- The hearing officer will cite the section of the master contract under which the meeting is being conducted.
- The hearing officer will specify the sequence in which the testimony will be presented.
- The principal will present all documentation to support the allegations of misconduct.
- The hearing officer will permit the staff member and the staff member's representative to cross-examine the principal and to present any pertinent documentation.
- The hearing officer will consider any explanation or extenuating situations that the staff member may present to explain his or her actions.
- If the staff member rambles, the hearing officer should interrupt the presentation rather than let the staff member ramble.
- The hearing officer will close the meeting by telling the staff member's representative that he or she will deliberate and then inform the parties of the recommendation.
- Before recommending a resolution, the hearing officer will assess and will reflect on the documentation and testimony presented at the meeting.
  - Has an act of misconduct happened?
  - Has a careful investigation been conducted to discover relevant facts about the misconduct allegation?

Evaluation of the Misconduct Decision

- The principal should recommend to the hearing officer disciplinary action consistent with that used for other staff members at the school or in the school district.
- The hearing officer will decide if the "preponderance of the evidence" will support the allegation(s) that probable cause exists that sexual misconduct did occur. If it does *not*, he or she will inform the staff member's representative that no further misconduct action will be taken.
- But if the evidence *does* support the allegation(s) that probable cause exists, he or she will inform the staff member's representative about the proposed disciplinary action to resolve the case.

Notification of the Staff Member

- Within the contractual timeline, the hearing officer will recommend a possible misconduct conclusion and call the staff member's representative.
- If the staff member's representative rejects the recommended resolution, the case will move to the next level of the misconduct process.
- If the staff member's representative and the staff member agree with the hearing officer's resolution, write a letter outlining the resolution for the staff member's file.

Next Misconduct Level—The Board of Education Hearing (See Chapter 10)

- If the staff member and the representative disagree with the hearing officer's proposed resolution, move to the board of education level of the misconduct process.
- If the board of education concurs with the recommendation of the hearing officer, the director of personnel sends a letter to the staff member and the representative informing them.

12

Abuse of
Controlled
Substances

*Control your temper during a misconduct hearing. Although you may
be under pressure, always demonstrate poise and self-control.*

For school districts, the number of staff members who have problems
with abuse of controlled substances is an increasing problem. Some
staff members abuse controlled substances such as use morphine, cocaine,
alcohol, codeine, heroine, barbiturates, and other depressants or hallucino-
gens. In fact, school districts have had to develop Employee Assistance
Programs (EAPs) to assist staff members. Still, despite the availability of
free counseling and therapy, many staff members who use controlled
substances do not seek help for their problem. As the principal, you must
be alert to the warning signs that the staff member has a problem with a
controlled substance. Some of the obvious signs are as follows:

- Mental confusion
- Loss of memory
- Distorted sense of one's ability to perform assigned duties
- Undependability at work
- Tendency to verbal outbursts around students and staff
- Loss of muscle control
- Slow speech
- Blank look on face

- Frequent colds or flu that result in absence and tardiness
- Runny nose
- Frequent sniffling
- Sudden weight loss
- Excessive swearing
- Smell of alcohol

Staff members who use these controlled substances may have a negative impact upon the learning atmosphere in the classroom. A staff member may react angrily toward students or other staff members if the desire for the controlled substance is unfulfilled. Also that staff member may be less productive in working with students and other staff. In addition, staff members who use controlled substances are more likely to have a high rate of absence or tardiness, which interferes with students' learning.

Moreover, staff members who use controlled substances may prevail upon colleagues to help them cover up or conceal their problems at work. If a colleague does not comply, the staff member often becomes resentful and unfriendly. This kind of unprofessional conduct cannot fail to interfere with the operation of the school.

Progressive Discipline Chart 12.1 provides examples of crimes and misconduct related to the abuse of controlled substances. You should research your school district's misconduct files to complete the progressive discipline chart for the first, second, third, and fourth violations.

When a staff member has been involved in a crime related to a controlled substance, you will need to respond decisively. For criminal misconduct involving a controlled substance, the following steps should be taken:

Speak to Personnel at the Central Administration Office Immediately

- Call your immediate supervisor.
- Call the public relations specialist for the district.
- Call the director of personnel for the district.
- If the three of you agree, call the police department which has jurisdiction in your school district.

Investigation

- Start an investigation relative to the criminal misconduct incident or assist the police who have jurisdiction in your school district to conduct the investigation.
- Use a standard form to collect statements from all witnesses and other individuals—including the parents—who may have information about the alleged incident. This may include students, staff, and secretaries. Written statements will help ensure that the information is more accurate and complete. (See Resource G.)
- Remind the witness and victims to be specific and to include the following:

Chart 12.1   **Progressive Discipline Chart 12.1—Abuse of Controlled Substances**

Controlled Substance Misconduct	First Violation	Second Violation	Third Violation	Fourth Violation
Being under the influence of alcohol at school	Immediate suspension			
Possession of drug paraphernalia				
Dealing drugs or drug paraphernalia in school				
Drunkenness on the job				
Giving a controlled substance to a student				
Possession of a controlled substance in a drug-free zone				
Possession of drugs in school				
Selling a controlled substance to students				
Unfit to work because of alcohol or drug use				
Possession and use of alcohol or illegal drugs while on duty				

Copyright © 2003 by Corwin Press, Inc. All rights reserved. Reprinted from *How to Handle Staff Misconduct, Second Edition* by C. Edward Lawrence and Myra K. Vachon. Reproduction authorized only for the local school site that has purchased this book.

- When (date and time)
- Where (location or area in which the incident occurred)
- Who (first and last names of people involved or who were witnesses, if known)
- What (events and actions that occurred)

• Interview witnesses separately and follow up with pointed questions. Probe witnesses to ensure that all information is accurate and complete.

• Thoroughly read statements to see if there are any contradictions, such as dates or times.

• If necessary, use the body diagram (Resource H) to show the part(s) of the body involved in this incident.

• If necessary, draw a diagram that shows where the incident occurred and any movement of persons involved.

• If necessary, use photographs or videotapes of the classroom or area where the incident occurred.

• Contact law enforcement agencies (e.g., police, sheriff, FBI), for a copy of the police report and statement of charges.

• Collect any supplemental documentation. This documentation may include board policy relative to the workday; staff handbook references, such as guidelines for student supervision and standards for staff; and weekly bulletin references to the Standards for Acceptable Conduct for Staff (see Resource A).

Past Misconduct Files

• To obtain information about progressive discipline, review the misconduct files in the school and the district administrative office.

• Before you recommend disciplinary action, review misconduct files to ensure that recommended disciplinary action fits the seriousness of the incident.

• Review the information collected during the investigation to determine whether the misconduct section of the master contract should be invoked.

• Review the district's misconduct database to find similar disciplinary actions against other staff members.

• Decide if your documentation supports the allegations of misconduct.

Preparation for the Misconduct
Meeting With the Hearing Officer (See Chapter 9)

• Send a letter to the staff member to schedule a meeting wherein you will discuss the information that might lead to allegations of misconduct.

• When you prepare documentation for the allegation of misconduct, place exhibits in the order you will present them.

• Prepare copies of all documentation for the staff member and the staff member's representative. Then distribute these at the meeting.

- Write out and practice aloud the opening statement for the meeting.
- Prepare personal notes to use during the meeting as a guide, but do not share those notes with the staff member or the staff member's representative.

Meeting Conducted by the Hearing Officer (See Resource J)

- Before the hearing officer begins the misconduct meeting, briefly introduce the participants.
- The hearing officer will ask the staff member to identify the person who is the official representative to speak at the meeting. If the staff member brings more than one person to the conference, only the official representative will be allowed to speak.
- The hearing officer will cite the section of the master contract under which the meeting is being conducted.
- The hearing officer will specify the sequence in which the testimony will be presented.
- The principal will present all documentation to support the allegations of misconduct.
- The hearing officer will permit the staff member and the staff member's representative to cross-examine and to present any pertinent documentation.
- The hearing officer will consider any explanation or extenuating situations that the staff member may present to explain his or her actions.
- If the staff member rambles, the hearing officer should interrupt the presentation rather than let the staff member ramble.
- The hearing officer will close the meeting by telling the staff member's representative that he or she will deliberate and then inform the parties of the recommendation.
- Before recommending a resolution, the hearing officer will assess and will reflect on the documentation and testimony presented at the meeting.
  - Has an act of misconduct happened?
  - Has a careful investigation been conducted to discover relevant facts about the misconduct allegation?

Evaluation of the Misconduct Decision

- The principal should recommend to the hearing officer disciplinary action consistent with that used for other staff members at the school or in the school district.
- The hearing officer will decide if the "preponderance of the evidence" will support the allegation(s) that probable cause exists that misconduct did occur. If it does *not*, he will inform the staff member's representative that no further misconduct action will be taken.
- But if the evidence *does* support the allegation(s) that probable cause exists, he will inform the staff member's representative about the proposed disciplinary action to resolve the case.

Notification of the Staff Member

- Within the contractual timeline, the hearing officer will recommend a possible misconduct conclusion and call the staff member's representative.
- If the staff member's representative rejects the recommended resolution, the case will move to the next level of the misconduct process.
- If the staff member's representative and the staff member agree with the hearing officer's resolution, write a letter outlining the resolution for the staff member's file.

Next Misconduct Level—The
Board of Education Hearing (See Chapter 10)

- If the staff member and the representative disagree with the hearing officer's proposed resolution, move to the board of education level of the misconduct process.
- If the board of education concurs with the recommendation of the hearing officer, the director of personnel sends a letter to the staff member and the representative informing them.

13

Theft and Fraud

Theft of school property or theft from a school fund can be a serious problem for school districts.

Another serious form of staff misconduct related to theft is fraud. Frequently, fraud is the abuse or misuse of sick leave time by staff members. As is so often the case, the successful pursuit of misconduct charges against a staff member requires that the principal keep, or supervise the keeping of, accurate records. Staff sick days must be recorded daily, periodically reviewed by staff members, and certified as accurate. Without such records, misconduct related to fraud in the use of sick time cannot be substantiated.

Because of the emphasis today on technology to teach children, staff members have a greater opportunity to be involved in incidents of theft. As the principal, you must have procedures in place to confirm purchase order numbers and to verify the date equipment was received at the school. Also, you must keep excellent records of equipment purchased, including the requisition or purchase order number, the date of order, the model number of the equipment, the price of the equipment, and the quantity ordered. Furthermore, it is also a very good procedure to take photographs or use a video camera to document the inventory of equipment, such as the school's audiovisual learning equipment, computers and related peripherals, shop equipment, VCRs, DVDs, TVs, and video cameras.

Of course, thieves may target the school and break in to steal this equipment, but staff members also take equipment from the school for personal use without authorization. When they fail to return it because records of the loan are not carefully maintained, the equipment is effectively stolen from the school, and other staff and students do not have the opportunity to avail themselves of the learning activities these items were purchased to provide. Education is actually affected when the principal fails to thoroughly and carefully maintain records, or oversee the keeping of records, of the equipment the school district has purchased.

Chart 13.1 is the progressive discipline chart that includes examples of fraud and theft misconduct. You should research your school district's misconduct files to complete the progressive discipline chart for the first, second, third, and fourth violations.

When you believe that a staff member or staff members may have committed a fraud or theft, you should follow the action steps below:

Speak to Personnel at the
Central Administration Office Immediately

- Call your immediate supervisor.
- Call the police department (to report the theft). You will not want to charge a staff member with a fraud or theft until an investigation has been completed.
- Call the public relations specialist for the district if a staff member is about to be charged with a crime by the police.
- Call the director of personnel for the district if a staff member will be charged by the police with a theft or fraud.

Investigation

- Start an investigation relative to the fraud or theft incident or assist the police who have jurisdiction in your school district to conduct the investigation.
- If the incident involves the theft of equipment, carefully review your records of the equipment and record all pertinent serial numbers, dates, and other information necessary to document a theft. Make copies to share with law enforcement authorities.
- If the incident involves a fraud, review, for example, the records of the extracurricular activities funds or the attendance records of sick days, to document the fraud. Consider making copies of the records for the investigation folder.
- Use a standard form to collect statements from all witnesses and other individuals—including the parents—who may have information about the alleged incident. This may include students, staff, and secretaries. This will help ensure that the information is more accurate and complete. (See Resource G.)
- Remind the witness and victims to be specific and to include the following:
  - When (date and time)
  - Where (location or area in which the incident occurred)
  - Who (first and last names of people involved or who were witnesses, if known)
  - What (events and actions that occurred)

Chart 13.1   Progressive Discipline Chart 13.1—Theft and Fraud

Theft and Fraud Misconduct	First Violation	Second Violation	Third Violation	Fourth Violation
Claiming extra assignment pay on days recorded as being sick	Immediate suspension	Termination		
Claiming unauthorized pay				
Claiming unauthorized sick time				
Conducting commercial business during school time				
Conducting personal business during school time				
Embezzling school funds				
Falsifying payroll records				
Forgery				
Misappropriating school funds				
Stealing money from a staff member				
Stealing money from the school beverage fund				
Stealing office supplies, books, utensils, etc., from the school				
Theft of audiovisual equipment (e.g., camcorders, radios, TV, VCR, DVD) or taking such items home for personal use without authorization				
Taking computer equipment from the school without authorization				
Unauthorized use of tax exemption number				
Working for another agency during school hours				

Copyright © 2003 by Corwin Press, Inc. All rights reserved. Reprinted from *How to Handle Staff Misconduct, Second Edition* by C. Edward Lawrence and Myra K. Vachon. Reproduction authorized only for the local school site that has purchased this book.

- Interview witnesses separately and follow up with pointed questions. Probe witnesses to ensure that all information is accurate and complete.
- Thoroughly read statements to see if there are any inconsistencies and contradictions, or inaccuracies, such as dates or correct times.
- If necessary, use the body diagram to show the part(s) of body involved in this incident (see Resource H).
- If necessary, draw a diagram that shows where the incident occurred and any movement of persons involved.
- If necessary, use photographs or videotapes of the classroom or area where the incident occurred.
- When the authorities have completed their investigations, contact the law enforcement agencies (e.g., police, sheriff, FBI), for a copy of their report and statement of charges.
- Collect any supplemental documentation. This documentation may include board policy relative to the workday; staff handbook references, such as guidelines for student supervision and standards for staff; and weekly bulletin references to the Standards for Acceptable Conduct for Staff (see Resource A).

Past Misconduct Files

- To obtain information about progressive discipline, review the misconduct files in the school and the district administrative office for the records of discipline used in similar misconduct incidents in the past.
- Before you recommend disciplinary action, review these misconduct files to ensure that your recommended disciplinary action is appropriate for the seriousness of the incident and consistent with past district disciplinary procedures.
- Review the information collected during the investigation to determine whether the misconduct section of the master contract should be invoked.
- Review the district's misconduct database to find similar disciplinary actions against other staff member.
- Decide if your documentation supports the allegations of misconduct.

Preparation for the Misconduct
Meeting With the Hearing Officer (See Chapter 9)

- Send a letter to the staff member to schedule a meeting wherein you will discuss the information related to the theft or fraud that might lead to allegations of misconduct.
- When you prepare documentation for the allegation of misconduct, place exhibits in the order you will present them.
- Prepare copies of all documentation for the staff member and the staff member's representative. Then distribute these at the meeting.
- Write out and practice aloud the opening statement for the meeting.

- Prepare personal notes to use as a guide during the meeting, but do not share those notes with the staff member or the staff member's representative.

The Meeting Conducted by
the Hearing Officer (See Resource J)

- When the hearing officer begins the misconduct meeting, briefly introduce participants.
- The hearing officer will ask the staff member to identify the person who is the official representative to speak at the meeting. If the staff member brings more than one person to the conference, only the official representative will be allowed to speak at the meeting.
- The hearing officer will cite the section of the master contract under which the meeting is being conducted.
- The hearing officer will specify the sequence in which the testimony will be presented.
- The principal will present all documentation related to the theft or fraud to support the allegations of misconduct.
- The hearing officer will permit the staff member and the staff member's representative to cross-examine and to present any pertinent documentation.
- The hearing officer will consider any new explanation or extenuating circumstances that the staff member may present to explain his or her actions.
- If the staff member rambles, the hearing officer should interrupt the presentation rather than let the staff member ramble.
- The hearing officer will close the meeting by telling the staff member's representative that he or she will need time to deliberate and the staff member and the representative will be informed of the recommendation.
- Before recommending a resolution, the hearing officer will assess and reflect upon the documentation and testimony presented at the meeting.
  - Does he or she honestly believe that an act of misconduct related to theft or fraud happened?
  - Has a careful investigation been conducted to obtain relevant facts about the allegation of theft or fraud?

Evaluation of the Misconduct Decision

- The hearing officer will recommend disciplinary action consistent with that used for other staff members at the school or in the school district.
- The hearing officer will decide if the "preponderance of the evidence" will support the allegation(s) that probable cause exists that misconduct did occur. If it does *not*, the hearing officer will

inform the staff member's representative that no further misconduct action will be taken.

- But if the evidence *does* support the allegation(s) that probable cause exists, the hearing officer will inform the staff member's representative about the proposed disciplinary action to resolve the case.

Notification of the Staff Member

- Within the contractual timeline, the hearing officer will recommend a possible misconduct conclusion; the hearing officer will call the staff member's representative.
- If the staff member's representative rejects the hearing officer's recommended resolution, the case will be moved to the next level of the misconduct process.
- If the staff member's representative and the staff member agree with the hearing officer's resolution, write a letter for the staff member's file summarizing the hearing officer's recommendation.

Next Misconduct Level—The Board of Education Hearing (See Chapter 10)

- If the staff member and the representative disagree with the hearing officer's proposed resolution, move the case to the board of education level of the misconduct process.
- If the board of education concurs with the recommendation for termination, the director of personnel will send a letter to the staff member and the representative informing them of the resolution of the grievance process.

14

Criminal Misconduct Outside the School Setting

As the principal, avoid social relationships with staff members, especially those that may involve drinking, such as house parties or going to a bar.

As the principal, you must be a good role model for your staff and students. In fact, all staff members are role models for students, both inside and outside of the school site. Staff members are held to a higher standard of conduct than are many other people in the community and are expected to conduct themselves in ways that set good examples for students. When a staff member sets a bad example for students, he or she can be dismissed from the school district if sufficient evidence indicates that the person may have engaged in outside conduct that would impair on-the-job effectiveness or working relationships with staff, students, and parents.

Unfortunately, from time to time, a staff member may commit a criminal act outside of the school that requires the involvement of the police department or another law enforcement agency. Some examples of outside criminal acts include murder, armed robbery, car theft, drug possession or use of illegal substances, possession of stolen items, and sexual activity involving a minor.

A staff member who is involved in criminal conduct outside the school setting may be imprisoned for a period of time. You must still hold a meeting immediately to suspend the teacher with pay within the contract time limit. Moreover, you must suspend the staff member without pay and then write a letter to postpone future misconduct meetings until the staff member is able attend the misconduct meeting.

Progressive Discipline Chart 14.1 has examples of criminal misconduct outside the school setting. You should research your school district's misconduct files to complete the progressive discipline chart for the first, second, third, and fourth violations.

When you believe that a staff member or staff members may have committed a criminal act, you should follow the action steps below:

Speak to Personnel at the
Central Administration Office Immediately

- Call your immediate supervisor.
- Call the police department (to report the crime). You will not want to charge a staff member with a crime until an investigation has been completed.
- Call the public relations specialist for the district if a staff member is about to be charged with a crime by the police.
- Call the director of personnel for the district if a staff member will be charged by the police with a crime.

Investigation

- Start an investigation relative to the misconduct incident or assist the police who have jurisdiction in your school district to conduct the investigation.
- Use a standard form to collect statements from all witnesses and other individuals—including the parents—who may have information about the alleged incident. This may include students, staff, and secretaries. This will help ensure that the information is more accurate and complete (see Resource G).
- Remind the witness and victims to be specific and to include the following:
  - When (date and time)
  - Where (location or area in which the incident occurred)
  - Who (first and last names of people involved or who were witnesses, if known)
  - What (events and actions that occurred)
- Interview witnesses separately and follow up with pointed questions. Probe witnesses to ensure that all information is accurate and complete.
- Thoroughly read statements to see if there are any inconsistencies and contradictions, or inaccuracies, such as dates or correct times.

Chart 14.1   Progressive Discipline Chart 14.1—Criminal Misconduct Outside the School Setting

Criminal Misconduct Outside of the School Site	First Violation	Second Violation	Third Violation	Fourth Violation
Arrested for being involved in a car theft ring				
Arrested for being involved in an attempt to commit murder				
Charged with participating in oral sex in a public restroom				
Arrested for being involved in an armed robbery				
Arrested for exposing students to sexually sensitive materials				
Arrested for making obscene gestures with a mannequin in public				
Arrested for public lewdness				
Arrested for taking nude photographs of students				
Charged with battery				
Charged with blackmail				
Charged with burglary				
Charged with counterfeiting				
Charged with credit card fraud				
Charged with engaging in sexual activities with minors				
Charged with gross disorderly conduct				
Charged with intent to commit rape				
Charged with masturbating in a public restroom				
Charged with possession of a controlled substance (e.g., cocaine, marijuana)				
Charged with possession of stolen property				
Charged with illegal use of explosives/firearms				
Providing alcohol to minors				

Copyright © 2003 by Corwin Press, Inc. All rights reserved. Reprinted from *How to Handle Staff Misconduct, Second Edition* by C. Edward Lawrence and Myra K. Vachon. Reproduction authorized only for the local school site that has purchased this book.

- If necessary, use the body diagram to show the part(s) of the body involved in this incident (see Resource H).
- If necessary, draw a diagram that shows where the incident occurred and any movement of persons involved.
- If necessary, use photographs or videotapes of the classroom or area where the incident occurred.
- When the authorities have completed their investigations, contact the law enforcement agencies (e.g., police, sheriff, FBI), for a copy of their report and statement of charges.
- Collect any supplemental documentation. This documentation may include board policy relative to the workday; staff handbook references, such as guidelines for student supervision and standards for staff; and weekly bulletin references to the Standards for Acceptable Conduct for Staff (see Resource A).

Past Misconduct Files

- To obtain information about progressive discipline, review the misconduct files in the school and the district administrative office for the records of discipline used in similar misconduct incidents in the past.
- Before you recommend disciplinary action, review these misconduct files to ensure that your recommended disciplinary action is appropriate for the seriousness of the incident and consistent with past district disciplinary procedures.
- Review the information collected during the investigation to determine whether the misconduct section of the master contract should be invoked.
- Review the district's misconduct database to find similar disciplinary actions against other staff members.
- Decide if your documentation supports the allegations of misconduct.

Preparation for the Misconduct
Meeting With the Hearing Officer (See Chapter 9)

- Send a letter to the staff member to schedule a meeting wherein you will discuss the information related to the crime that might lead to allegations of misconduct.
- When you prepare documentation for the allegation of misconduct, place exhibits in the order you will present them.
- Prepare copies of all documentation for the staff member and the staff member's representative. Then distribute these at the meeting.
- Write out and practice aloud the opening statement for the meeting.
- Prepare personal notes to use as a guide during the meeting, but do not share those notes with the staff member or the staff member's representative.

The Meeting Conducted by
the Hearing Officer (See Resource J)

- When the hearing officer begins the misconduct meeting, briefly introduce participants.
- The hearing officer will ask the staff member to identify the person who is the official representative to speak at the meeting. If the staff member brings more than one person to the conference, only the official representative will be allowed to speak at the meeting.
- The hearing officer will cite the section of the master contract under which the meeting is being conducted.
- The hearing officer will specify the sequence in which the testimony will be presented.
- The principal will present all documentation related to the crime to support the allegations of misconduct.
- The hearing officer will permit the staff member and the staff member's representative to cross-examine and to present any pertinent documentation.
- The hearing officer will consider any new explanation or extenuating circumstances that the staff member may present to explain his or her actions.
- If the staff member rambles, the hearing officer should interrupt the presentation rather than let the staff member ramble.
- The hearing officer will close the meeting by telling the staff member's representative that he or she will need time to deliberate and the staff member and the representative will be informed of the recommendation.
- Before recommending a resolution, the hearing officer will assess and reflect upon the documentation and testimony presented at the meeting.
  - Does he or she honestly believe that an act of misconduct related to a crime happened?
  - Has a careful investigation been conducted to obtain relevant facts about the allegation of a crime?

Evaluation of the Misconduct Decision

- The hearing officer will recommend disciplinary action consistent with that used for other staff members at the school or in the school district.
- The hearing officer will decide if the "preponderance of the evidence" will support the allegation(s) that probable cause exists that misconduct did occur. If it does *not*, the hearing officer will inform the staff member's representative that no further misconduct action will be taken.
- But if the evidence *does* support the allegation(s) that probable cause exists, the hearing officer will inform the staff member's representative about the proposed disciplinary action to resolve the case.

Notification of the Staff Member

- Within the contractual timeline, the hearing officer will recommend a possible misconduct resolution; the hearing officer will call the staff member's representative.
- If the staff member's representative rejects the hearing officer's recommended resolution, the case will be moved to the next level of the misconduct process.
- If the staff member's representative and the staff member agree with the hearing officer's resolution, write a letter for the staff member's file summarizing the hearing officer's recommendation.

Next Misconduct Level—The
Board of Education Hearing (See Chapter 10)

- If the staff member and the representative disagree with the hearing officer's proposed resolution, move the case to the board of education level of the misconduct process.
- If the board of education concurs with the recommendation for termination, the director of personnel will send a letter to the staff member and the representative informing them of the resolution of the grievance process.

Resources

Resource A

Standards of Acceptable Conduct for Staff Members

To ensure the efficient, orderly operation of the school and to provide a safe learning environment for students, all staff members are expected to conduct themselves in a professional manner. These standards include but are not limited to the standards listed below for all staff members:

1. Report to work on time and refrain from leaving before the established time.

2. Perform assigned duties.

3. Attend staff meetings.

4. Follow reasonable administrative directives.

5. Refrain from engaging in sexual harassment of students or staff.

6. Refrain from any sexual contact or conduct with students.

7. Refrain from using abusive, profane, and/or insulting language toward students.

8. Refrain from coming to work under the influence of alcohol or drugs or being in possession of a controlled substance.

9. Refrain from leaving students unsupervised.

10. Refrain from excessive use of the school telephone, computer, or fax machine for personal use.

11. Refrain from removing any school-owned equipment or supplies without the principal's written authorization.

12. Refrain from sleeping while supervising children.

13. Refrain from using corporal punishment as defined by state statutes and by board of education policy.

14. Refrain from using racial slurs toward students or other staff members.

15. Maintain a professional working relationship with other staff members at all times.

16. Refrain from arguing or fighting with another staff member in the presence of students.

17. Refrain from distributing any flyers or other materials that are profane, vulgar, or that have racial or gender slurs.

18. Refrain from conducting personal or nonschool business during the workday.

19. Refrain from using for profit your position or influence over students.

20. Refrain from bringing guns or weapons to school.

If a staff member fails to comply with the standards of acceptable conduct expected at work, including but not limited to the foregoing examples, the staff member may be subject to disciplinary action.

Resource B

Letter to Schedule an Oral Reprimand Conference

November 12, 20XX

Mr. William Anthony
397 West Jackson Circle
Crescent Ridge, CA 70799

Dear Mr. Anthony:

I would like to meet with you as soon as possible to discuss an alleged incident involving you. Please see my schedule to arrange a conference this week.

Yours truly,

Lemmie Wade, Ph.D.
Principal
cc: Darren L. Miller, Representative, ABC Educators' Association

Resource C

Major Components of an Oral Warning

Date	September 6, 20XX
Time	3:15 P.M.
Location	Room 214
Individuals present	Mr. Anthony and principal
Tell the individual about the concern	"Mr. Anthony, your students are not being picked up from the cafeteria on time. Your students have to wait for you after the other teachers have all picked up their students. I'm concerned about this. Can you help me solve this problem?"
Listen with an open mind	"I guess I have a problem with being on time to pick up my students. I know I have to do better. I go home to eat lunch and get caught up in traffic. I find myself speeding to get back to school and then I run to the other side of the building to pick up my students, and I'm late. I'm sorry. I know I've got to improve."
Ask the individual if he or she can help you	"What can you do to help me resolve my concern about your students not being picked up on time? Is there anything you can do to help me?"
Listen to the staff member	"Yes, I can. It won't happen again."
Ask questions	"Do you have any questions about what I need you to do?"

Listen

Let the staff member know what is expected and what will happen if a similar offense occurs in the future

"Mr. Anthony, I want to be as clear as possible about my concerns about your picking up your students on time from the buses in the morning, after recess, and after lunch times, and then escorting them quietly back to class. I really need your help to try to reduce the school problems during that time. Can I count on you? From this day on, any future problems with your picking up your students on time will result in disciplinary action."

Farewell

"Good evening."

Resource D

Letter to Schedule a Misconduct Meeting

ABC School District
Kennedy Elementary School
1584 South Pineview Drive
Crescent Ridge, CA 70799
(916) 444–8888

October 4, 20XX

Mr. William Anthony
397 West Jackson Circle
Crescent Ridge, CA 70799

Dear Mr. Anthony:

This letter is to notify you that allegations of misconduct have been made against you that may lead to disciplinary action.

A meeting is scheduled on Friday, October 6, 20XX, at 3:30 P.M. in my office to discuss these allegations. You are entitled to be represented at this conference by the ABC Educators' Association or legal counsel to ensure that due process is followed according to the master contract.

Yours truly,

Lemmie Wade, Ph.D.
Principal
cc: Darren L. Miller, Representative, ABC Educators' Association

Resource E

First Letter of Reprimand—Major Components

Step 1. The reprimand letter must be on official school letterhead.

ABC School District
Kennedy Elementary School
584 South Pineview Drive
Crescent Ridge, CA 70799
(916) 444–8888

October 27, 20XX
Certified mail, school mail, or hand delivered (method of transmittal)

Mr. William Anthony
397 West Jackson Circle
Crescent Ridge, CA 70799

Dear Mr. Anthony:

Step 2. Describe the incident precisely: involvement of individual, date, time, and location.

At 3:30 P.M. on Thursday, October 23, 20XX, I met with you in my office to issue an oral reprimand with regard to my concern about _____ (specify the misconduct, such as neglect of duty). This letter of reprimand is written documentation about the concerns I expressed to you on October 23. Listed below are the reasons I am issuing this letter (list the reasons as in the examples below):

  – You are frequently late reporting to duty.
  – You take extended morning coffee breaks in teachers' lounge.
  – You use the school phone excessively for personal business.
  – You take extended lunch breaks beyond the contractual limit of 30 minutes.

Step 3. Quote the regulation(s) that was broken.

The above are clear violations of the master contract and the Standards of Acceptable Behavior for Staff Members (see Resource A) while at work. According to Part III, Section 3 of the master contract, "_____" (state the provision). Moreover, number _____ (state the number) in the

Standards of Acceptable Behavior for Staff Members clearly states as follows: "_____" (Quote from the Standards).

Step 4. Include all dates of previous oral or written warnings issued throughout the school year. Be specific about the occurrences, including dates.

I warned you several times this semester of my concerns about (specify misconduct). Specifically, I told you about (specify acts and events like those following) being tardy for duty on Wednesday, September 6; Friday, September 8; and Tuesday, September 12, 20XX. On Friday, September 8, 20XX, I gave you a verbal warning that you must report to duty on time to perform your required task. Nonetheless, you were late to duty again Monday, October 11; Tuesday, October 12; and Friday, October 15.

Step 5. Mention any assistance you offered including suggestions as to how the person could improve.

I asked you if you needed any assistance to get to your duty on time. You said "No." I suggested you purchase a wristwatch with an alarm so you would be on time for your duty.

Step 6. State that the letter is a written reprimand.

Because you have not heeded my previous warnings to correct your (specify misconduct), this letter of written reprimand is a disciplinary step.

Step 7. Explain to the staff member that he or she has one more opportunity to improve conduct and you hope that he or she will.

With this letter, I am offering you one more opportunity to improve, and I hope you will.

Step 8. Explain that if the employee does not show improvement, he or she will be subject to further disciplinary action.

You must correct the abuses we discussed: (specify acts of misconduct like those following) long morning coffee breaks in the teachers' lounge, excessive use of the school phone for personal business, extending your lunch break beyond the contractual 30-minute time limit, and late in reporting to duty. If you do not correct these abuses, you will be subject to additional disciplinary action.

Step 9. Close the letter of reprimand.

Yours truly,

Lemmie Wade, Ph.D.
School Principal
cc: Personnel file
Dawn M. Fitzgerald, Chief Personnel Director, ABC School District
Darren L. Miller, Representative, ABC Educators' Association
This is to verify that I have received this letter.
Signature: _____ Date: _____

Resource F

Second Letter of Reprimand—Major Components

Step 1. The reprimand letter must be on official school letterhead.

ABC School District
Kennedy Elementary School
584 South Pineview Drive
Crescent Ridge, CA 70799
(916) 444–8888

November 27, 20XX
Certified mail, school mail, or hand delivered (method of transmittal)

Mr. William Anthony
397 West Jackson Circle
Crescent Ridge, CA 70799

Dear Mr. Anthony:

Step 2. Reprimand letter must be precise with reference to the individual involvement, date, time, and witnesses to the incident.

This second letter of reprimand is being sent to you because of my continued concern regarding _____ (specify the misconduct, such as neglect of duty). In the first letter, I informed you about the reasons for the initial reprimand: (list the reasons, such as those that follow): frequently late reporting to duty; extended morning coffee breaks in teachers' lounge; excessive use of school phone for personal use; and extended lunch break beyond the contractual 30-minute limit. For the reasons listed below, you are again being reprimanded in this second letter for continued _____ (specify the misconduct, such as neglect of duty):

- Frequently late reporting to duty
- Taking extended morning coffee breaks in teachers' lounge
- Failing to escort students to cafeteria
- Failing to pick up students after recess and lunch

Step 3. Quote the regulation(s) that was broken.

As I stated in the first letter of reprimand, these are clear violations of the master contract and the Standards of Acceptable Behavior for Staff

Members (see Resource A) while at work. I want to reiterate that the master contract between the board of education and the ABC Educators' Association states the following: (Quote the contract and quote the Standards of Acceptable Behavior.)

> *Step 4. Refer to all dates of previous oral or written warnings given out to the employee throughout the school year. Be specific about what you saw or heard.*

As I stated in the first letter of reprimand, you were warned of my concerns about your _____ (specify misconduct) several times this semester. Specifically, I told you about _____ (specify acts of misconduct like those following) being tardy for duty on Wednesday, September 6; Friday, September 8; and Tuesday, September 12, 20XX. On Friday, September 8, 20XX, I gave you a friendly warning to report to duty on time to perform your duties. You were late to duty again Monday, October 11; Tuesday, October 12; and Friday, October 15.

I am concerned that you have continued to neglect your duties at work. I issued you a letter of reprimand dated October 27, 20XX, for failure to escort your students to the cafeteria. I warned you that you must escort your students to the lunchroom, and I reiterated that all staff members are required to follow the Standards of Acceptable Behavior for Staff Members at work. Number 9 says that staff members are to "refrain from leaving students unsupervised." I also suggested that you read the Staff Handbook, pages 21 through 29, which explains the procedures for the proper supervision of students.

> *Step 5. Mention any assistance or ideas on how to improve.*

During the first reprimand meeting, I asked you if you needed any assistance to get to your duty on time. You said "No." I suggested you purchase a wristwatch with an alarm in order to get to your duty on time. Again, I asked you if you needed any assistance, and you said, "I can get to duty on time and do not need any help."

> *Step 6. State that the letter is an official letter of reprimand.*

This letter serves as a second official letter of reprimand for _____ (specify the misconduct, such as neglect of duty, and list specific days and times).

> *Step 7. Explain to the staff member the penalty for failure to improve performance.*

Since you have failed to follow previous oral warnings and my first letter of reprimand, I recommend that you be suspended without pay for one day. I want to state as emphatically as possible that you are responsible for supervising your students at all times during the school day.

Step 8. Explain that if there is no improvement, the employee will be subject to further disciplinary action.

You will be subject to more disciplinary action up to and including termination from the ABC School District if you fail to correct the (specify the misconduct).

Step 9. Invite the employee to state his or her view on the matter in writing.

According to the master contract, you can respond to this letter in writing within five (5) workdays of its receipt. Your letter will be attached to the letter placed in your personnel file.

Step 10. Remind the employee of grievance and other appeal procedures that are available.

The master contract has a provision that allows you to appeal your one-day suspension within the ten (10) school days.

Step 11. Closure of Letter of Reprimand.

Yours truly,

Lemmie Wade, Ph.D.
School Principal
cc: Dawn M. Fitzgerald, Chief Personnel Director, ABC School District
Darren L. Miller, Representative, ABC Educators' Association

Resource G

Allegation of Staff Misconduct
Standard Report Form

Report Date: _____ Date of Incident:_____

Name of Accused Staff Member: _____

School: _____

Time of Incident: _____ Location of Incident: _____

Location where statement was taken: _____

I, _____, am a student/staff member at _____
      (name)   (circle one)

School, located at _____.
                 (address, city, state)

I am making this statement to _____, principal of

_____ School, in the presence of _____,

assistant principal, and _____, school secretary.

STATEMENT

_____
_____
_____
_____
_____
_____
_____
_____
_____
_____
_____
_____
_____
_____
_____
_____
_____
_____
_____
_____
_____
_____
_____
_____
_____
_____
_____

Initials of Victim: _____ Date: _____

page number _____ of _____ pages

The school principal has read the above statement consisting of _____ pages to me. I initialed and dated each page of the report. I further certify that I initialed corrections in this statement. To the best of my firsthand knowledge of this incident, the above statement is the truth.

Signature of Victim: _____

Date: _____   Time: _____

OR

Signature of Witness: _____

Date: _____   Time: _____

Signature of School Principal: _____

Date: _____   Time: _____

Resource H

Diagram of Human Body

To present precise information about the area of the body involved in an incident, use the body diagram on the following page. The victim or witness should mark an "X" in the circle and put their initials next to it.

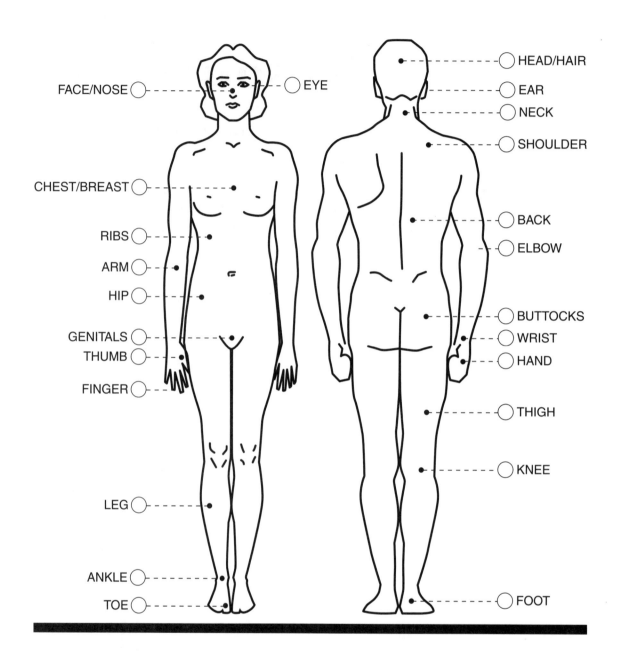

Resource I

Misconduct Meeting at the School Level

Greeting and introduction if you do not know the staff member's representative	"Good afternoon. I don't believe we've met. I'm Lemmie Wade, the principal of Kennedy Elementary School. This is Henry Felton, my assistant principal. He will attend this meeting to take notes."
Acknowledgment of contractual provision and due process	"We are proceeding under Section III, paragraph (A) of the master contract. These misconduct provisions ensure substantive and procedural due process. This afternoon I will present evidence with regard to allegations of misconduct against William Anthony."
Sequence of testimony at meeting	"First, I will present my evidence. After my presentation, you will have an opportunity to present your evidence on behalf of Mr. Anthony, or you may cross-examine me about the evidence I present."
Clarification of procedure	"Do you have any questions about how this meeting will proceed? If not, we will begin the meeting."
Opening statement	"Because our most important obligation is to provide for the safety of our students, all staff members are important in the operation of Kennedy Elementary School. In order to help achieve this goal, I expect all staff members to abide by the rules of the board of education, the master contract, and the school's procedures and guidelines, and this is especially important where safety is concerned. Moreover, state statutes empower me to do what is necessary to ensure staff members carry out their responsibilities, including supervision of students. I will show that Mr. Anthony received an oral warning, an oral reprimand, a follow-up memo, and a written letter of reprimand. But he has continually failed to carry out his duty to supervise students when scheduled to do so."

References to due process	"At the beginning of the school year, August 20, 20XX, I informed all staff members of the school procedures and guidelines stated in the Standards of Acceptable Conduct, which apply to all staff members. I have not singled out any staff member. Therefore, when Mr. Anthony's conduct violates school procedures and guidelines, I must invoke the misconduct section of the master contract to resolve the issue."
Background information about the teacher	"Mr. Anthony has been a teacher in the ABC School District since August 2000, when he started teaching at King Middle School. At the beginning of the 20XX school year, he transferred to Kennedy Elementary School. At that time, I did not find misconduct letters in either his district personnel or his King Middle School file. However, while Mr. Anthony taught at Kennedy Elementary School this year, he received an oral warning, an oral reprimand with a follow-up memo, and a letter of reprimand."
State nature of allegation	"I have proof of each allegation, with supportive evidence. These allegations against Mr. Anthony are all violations of the Standards of Acceptable Conduct and will be discussed individually: • Frequently late reporting to duty • Taking extended morning coffee breaks in the teacher's lounge • Failing to pick up students after lunch and after recess Mr. Anthony's behavior creates a safety issue and is detrimental to students, staff, and the school."
Distribute copy of documentation	"I am distributing to you a folder that contains a copy of the documentation that I will present during this meeting. Each item is labeled as an exhibit."
Presenting your evidence	"On August 28, 20XX, the first school day, all staff members received a copy of the Standards of Acceptable Conduct for Staff Members. I thoroughly discussed each standard with the staff and also asked if anyone had questions or wanted additional explanation. Mr. Anthony did not respond. I now present Exhibit A—Standards of Acceptable Conduct for Staff Members.

"By leaving students unsupervised, Mr. Anthony has violated Standard 9. Mr. Anthony was late five minutes picking up his students August 29 and six minutes late on September 2. On Tuesday, September 3, I told him about my concern and that I needed his help to resolve the problem. This was his oral warning.

"Then on September 6, Mr. Anthony was eight minutes late. Ten students were referred to my office that day for fighting after lunch. At that time, I told Mr. Anthony that when he fails to pick students up on time from the playground, it can lead to student fights. This was his oral reprimand, and I am presenting Exhibit B, which is the follow-up memo to Mr. Anthony."

Continue to present all evidence at the first meeting to substantiate the allegations of misconduct, including labeled exhibits such as the master contract, state laws, staff bulletins, signed statements from parents, and records of parental complaints. It is important to do this at the first meeting because you may be unable to introduce new evidence at meetings that may follow.

Cross-examination	You must allow the teacher's representative an opportunity to present evidence on the teacher's behalf and to cross-examine you about the evidence you presented.
Closing statement by staff member's representative	Request the teacher's representative to make a closing statement.
Close the meeting with notice of intent to review	"In closing, I intend to review the information presented at the meeting and to adhere to the contractual timeline. Then I will telephone to give your representative my recommendations for the resolution of this misconduct situation."
Reference to contractual timeline	"According to the master contract, I must respond within seven workdays, but I will contact you before the end of next week."
Clarification of next step	"Do you have any questions?"
Farewell	"Good afternoon."

Next step—call representative

Call the staff member's representative about the proposed disciplinary action for this misconduct situation. If the staff member's representative disagrees with your proposal, the school district may choose from one of the first two options below or move the case to the next step outlined in the misconduct section of the master contract, with option 3 or 4.

Principal's options to resolve misconduct

1. Take no disciplinary action against the staff member.

2. Reduce the recommended disciplinary action.

3. Retain the staff member on staff but refer the misconduct matter to an impartial hearing officer.

4. Place the staff member on leave and refer the misconduct matter to an impartial hearing officer.

Resource J

Misconduct Meeting With Hearing Officer

Hearing officer's greeting	"Good afternoon. I am Dr. Jonathon Maximus, the hearing officer for this misconduct meeting."
State purpose of meeting	"The purpose of this meeting is to hear allegations of misconduct against Mr. Anthony."
Acknowledgment of contractual provision and due process	"According to Section III of the master contract, the next step in a misconduct case is that, under Provision III-C, an impartial hearing officer presides at this misconduct meeting, listens to testimony, and reviews documentation and evidence before rendering a recommended resolution."
Hearing officer gives the rules for meeting	"In order to reach this goal, it is important that all parties refrain from outburst and the use of abusive, insulting, or profane language. There must be no disruptions during the other person's presentation. Only one person will speak at a time.
	"Dr. Wade will present her testimony first. Next, the teacher's representative may cross-examine Dr. Wade, present documentation on behalf of the teacher, or ask Dr. Wade questions about her presentation. Do you have questions? If not, Dr. Wade, you may begin."
Principal's opening statement	"Thank you, Dr. Maximus. All staff members are important in the operation of Kennedy Elementary School. Our first obligation is to provide a safe environment for our students. In order to accomplish that goal, all staff members must adhere to Board of Education rules; the master contract; and the procedures, rules, regulations, and guidelines of our school."

Principal makes reference to due process

"At the beginning of the school year, August 20, 20XX, all staff members were informed about school procedures and guidelines at Kennedy Elementary School. Moreover, the same Standards of Acceptable Conduct at work have been applied to all staff members. In fact, no staff member has been singled out. The proposed resolution to this problem is consistent with the treatment of other staff members who were disciplined for similar actions and under similar circumstances. Because Mr. Anthony's conduct violates school procedures and guidelines, I must invoke the misconduct section of the master contract to resolve the problem."

Background information about the teacher

"Mr. Anthony has been a teacher in the ABC School District since August 2000, at which time he started teaching at King Middle School. At the beginning of the 20XX school year, he transferred to Kennedy Elementary School. I did not find misconduct letters in Mr. Anthony's district personnel or in his King Middle School file. But since Mr. Anthony has taught at Kennedy Elementary, he has received an oral warning, an oral reprimand, a follow-up memo, and a written letter of reprimand.

"On August 28, 20XX, the first school day, the staff received a copy of the Standards of Acceptable Conduct for Staff Members. I thoroughly discussed each standard and also asked if anyone had questions or wanted additional explanation. Mr. Anthony did not respond. I now present Exhibit A—Standards of Acceptable Conduct for Staff Members.

"By leaving students unsupervised, Mr. Anthony has violated Standard 9. Mr. Anthony was late five minutes picking up his students August 29 and six minutes late on September 2. On Tuesday, September 3, I told him about my concern and that I needed his help to resolve the problem. This was his oral warning.

"Then on September 6, Mr. Anthony was eight minutes late. Ten students were referred to my office that day for fighting after lunch. At that time, I told Mr. Anthony that when he fails to pick students up on time from the playground, it can lead to student fights. This was his oral reprimand, and I am presenting Exhibit B, which is the follow-up memo to Mr. Anthony."

Principal concisely states the misconduct allegations

"Allegations of misconduct are made against Mr. Anthony for the following reasons:
• Frequently late reporting to duty
• Taking extended morning coffee breaks in the teacher's lounge
• Failing to pick up students after lunch and after recess"

Principal restates each allegation of misconduct

"I will present documentation to support the first allegation: frequently late reporting to duty."

Principal provides supportive documentation

What happened (describe the incident)?
Date of incident
Time of incident

"Now, I will distribute Exhibit C—the Witness/Victim Form."

(Repeat above for each allegation.)

Principal summarizes statement

Briefly summarize allegations of misconduct. Then make a recommendation to resolve the misconduct incident.

Staff member's representative cross-examination

At this point, the staff member's representative will cross-examine you about your testimony.

Hearing officer request for closing statements

"First, the teacher representative will present a closing statement. Then Dr. Wade will present her closing statement. Each closing statement will have a two-minute time limit."

Principal presents closing statement—the clincher

"Thank you, Dr. Maximus. I believe that the documentation I presented this afternoon supports the allegation of misconduct in that Mr. Anthony has been neglectful of his duties. Moreover, proposed resolutions to these allegations are consistent with treatment of other staff members who were disciplined for similar actions under similar circumstances. I recommend that Mr. Anthony be suspended for one week without pay because of his continuous violation of state statutes, school board policy, the master contract, and the Standards of Acceptable Conduct for Staff Members."

Hearing officer closes the meeting with notice of intent to review

"In closing, I intend to review the information presented at the meeting and to adhere to the contractual timeline. Then I will telephone to give your representative my recommendations as to the resolution to this misconduct situation."

Hearing officer makes reference to contractual timeline

"According to the master contract, I must respond within seven workdays, but I will contact you before the end of next week."

Hearing officer gives clarification of the next step

"Do you have any questions?"

Farewell

"Good afternoon."

Hearing officer's options to resolve misconduct

1. Notify the staff member's representative that the recommendation for disciplinary action has been dropped, and no further action will be taken.

2. Notify the staff member's representative that the recommendation for disciplinary action has been reduced.

3. Notify the staff member's representative that the staff member may return to work during further misconduct proceedings.

4. Notify the staff member's representative that the hearing has been delayed because of a required court hearing or summer break.

5. Notify the staff member's representative that suspension without pay will continue throughout further misconduct proceedings.

6. Notify the staff member that the impartial hearing officer concurs with the principal's recommendation.

Hearing officer makes a courtesy call to staff member's representative

The hearing officer will call the staff member's representative about the proposed disciplinary action for this misconduct situation.

If the staff member's representative disagrees with the proposal, the case will move to the next step outlined in the misconduct section of the master contract.

Hearing officer sends a letter to confirm the recommended resolution.

Department of personnel involvement

1. Notify the staff member of the recommendation for termination for misconduct

2. Notify the staff member that the superintendent of schools concurs with the recommendation for termination.

3. Specify the misconduct charge(s), and schedule a conference of the board of education to serve as the impartial hearing body

4. Notify the staff member about the board decision. The board of education may reduce disciplinary action, drop the charges and reinstate the teacher, or concur with the recommendation for termination.

Resource K

Letter to the Media About Criminal Misconduct

When a staff member is involved in a criminal act inside or outside of the school setting, the news media may want information about the incident. Therefore, you must work with the school district's media specialist to prepare a press release for the news media, parents, students, and the community.

This will be a stressful time for all concerned, but you must work with the media in a spirit of cooperation. Make every effort to return their telephone calls immediately. Do not get into an argument with reporters, and while you might like to avoid saying "no comment" to them, you must be very cautious about the answers you give to their questions. You want the news media to present an accurate report, but you may not know all the facts surrounding the incident and it is important to maintain the confidentiality of personnel matters.

You should immediately decide if the incident is serious enough to hold a short meeting to inform your staff so they do not read about it from media sources.

In the press release, explain that personnel matters are confidential, and you are required to follow the provisions of the master contract to ensure due process.

On the next page is a sample of a press release for the news media, parents, students, and staff members.

Press Release
Staff Member Involved in a Criminal Act

ABC School District
Kennedy Elementary School
584 South Pineview Drive
Crescent Ridge, CA 70799
(916) 444–8888

November 12, 20XX

Today the police department arrested a teacher at Kennedy Elementary School at 10:45 A.M. The staff member is suspended from all duties. A substitute teacher has assumed the teaching responsibilities. Personnel issues are confidential matters; therefore, I am unable to provide you with any details about this incident.

The ABC Teachers' Association and the school district's contractual agreement requires due process protection rights for the staff member. Therefore, contractual provisions are followed to ensure due process rights.

Thank you.
Lemmie D. Wade, PhD
Principal

References

Enterprise Wire Company v. Enterprise Independent Union, 46 LA 359, 1966 (Arbitration case, 1966). Retrieved April 23, 2002, from http://homepages. uhwo.hawaii.edu/clear/EnterpriseWire.html

LaMorte, M. W. (2002). *School Law Cases and Concepts.* Boston: Allyn & Bacon.

Lawrence, C. E., & Vachon, M. K. (2001). *The Marginal Teacher: A Step-by-Step Guide to Fair Procedures for Identification and Dismissal.* Thousand Oaks, CA: Corwin.

Index

**CORWIN
PRESS**

The Corwin Press logo—a raven striding across an open book—represents the happy union of courage and learning. We are a professional-level publisher of books and journals for K-12 educators, and we are committed to creating and providing resources that embody these qualities. Corwin's motto is "Success for All Learners."